Empowering Small Businesses For Tomorrow

Empowering Small Businesses For Tomorrow

Ehsan Sheroy

UNIEK ENTERPRISES

CONTENTS

INDEX

Chapter 7: Financial Support and Resources
7.1 Access to Capital: Loans, Grants, and Investments
7.2 Financial Education for Small Business Owners
7.3 The Role of Governments and Financial Institutions

Chapter 8: Nurturing Entrepreneurship
8.1 Entrepreneurship Education and Training
8.2 Mentorship Programs and Incubators
8.3 Cultivating a Culture of Innovation and Creativity

Chapter 9: The Future of Small Businesses
9.1 The Ongoing Transformation of Local Economies
9.2 Innovations and Technological Advancements
9.3 The Road Ahead: Sustaining Small Businesses for Tomorrow

Chapter 1

Introduction

In a world set apart by consistent change and development, private ventures assume a crucial part in the worldwide economy. These undertakings are much of the time the foundation of neighborhood networks and contribute altogether to monetary development and advancement. They address the enterprising soul of society and are fundamental drivers of occupation creation, pay age, and abundance appropriation. Notwithstanding, regardless of their intrinsic significance, independent companies regularly face a variety of difficulties that can frustrate their development and manageability. In this presentation, we set out on an excursion to investigate the idea of "Enabling Private companies For Later."

Independent companies, characterized by their size, are ordinarily described by restricted assets, obliged financial plans, and a consistent need to adjust to changing economic situations. Their size permits them to be coordinated, inventive, and receptive to client needs, however it likewise implies that they frequently work on the edge of endurance, confronting obstacles like deficient admittance to funding, restricted mechanical abilities, and savage contest from bigger organizations.

The significance of independent ventures to the worldwide economy couldn't possibly be more significant. They act as fundamental wellsprings of work, contributing essentially to work creation, which is particularly crucial in a world wrestling with joblessness and underemployment. These organizations empower neighborhood networks to flourish, giving special items and administrations, encouraging a feeling of local area, and supporting different, reasonable economies. Independent ventures are monetary elements as well as basic pieces of the social texture.

Moreover, independent ventures are much of the time center points of advancement and innovative soul. Their deftness and versatility empower them to rapidly distinguish and immediately take advantage of chances. Numerous troublesome advancements and weighty arrangements have their underlying foundations in little, enterprising endeavors. By enabling independent ventures, we open a strong power for development and financial development, eventually molding the business scene of tomorrow.

However, notwithstanding their importance, private companies face a progression of fundamental difficulties that undermine their reality. Admittance to fund, for instance, is a common deterrent. Monetary organizations are frequently hesitant to give advances to independent ventures because of seen dangers and intricacies related with their tasks. This absence of admittance to capital can seriously restrict their development and advancement potential.

Another test that independent companies face is the fast speed of innovative headway. As digitalization and computerization keep on changing enterprises, independent companies frequently battle to keep up. Restricted spending plans and mastery impede their capacity to put resources into and take on state of the art innovations, which can prompt a cutthroat hindrance.

Additionally, private companies experience administrative weights and regulatory obstacles that can smother their development and efficiency. The complicated snare of consistence and administrative noise can be overpowering, especially for those with restricted assets and ability. This present circumstance frequently leaves entrepreneurs feeling caught and unfit to extend or enhance.

The serious scene is likewise overwhelming. Private companies frequently wind up in direct rivalry with huge organizations, which have the scale, assets, and advertising ability to outsmart them. This opposition can bring about a power lopsidedness that is hard for private companies to survive.

In this unique circumstance, the idea of "Engaging Private companies For Later" takes on essential importance. Strengthening alludes to the most common way of outfitting private ventures with the devices, assets, and backing they need to conquer these difficulties, flourish, and secure their position later on business scene. About establishing an empowering climate cultivates development, work creation, and monetary flexibility.

Strengthening envelops a few aspects. One of the most basic perspectives is giving independent companies better admittance to monetary assets. By guaranteeing that they can get the fundamental capital for development and advancement, we can eliminate one of the main obstructions to their prosperity. This incorporates conventional bank credits as well as elective funding choices like investment, crowdfunding, and microloans.

One more element of strengthening is upgrading private ventures' innovative abilities. Innovation is at the center of current business tasks, from advanced showcasing and web based business to information examination and computerization. Independent ventures need backing and direction to really embrace and influence these advances.

Additionally, administrative disentanglement and backing are fundamental parts of strengthening. By smoothing out regulatory cycles and offering direction and help, legislatures can lessen the managerial weight on private ventures and permit them to zero in on their center exercises.

Strengthening likewise includes making a level battleground by tending to the difficulties presented by bigger enterprises. This could incorporate antitrust guidelines, advancing fair rivalry, and setting out open doors for independent ventures to team up and shape associations that can support their seriousness.

Besides, building a hearty biological system of help is basic to private venture strengthening. This incorporates business warning administrations, mentorship programs, and systems administration amazing open doors. By interfacing entrepreneurs with experienced guides and companions, we can encourage a culture of learning and sharing prescribed procedures.

Notwithstanding these pragmatic parts of strengthening, cultivating a strong and comprehensive business climate is similarly significant. It implies perceiving the remarkable commitments of private ventures and recognizing their job in neighborhood and worldwide economies. Advancing mindfulness and enthusiasm for private ventures can prompt more noteworthy customer backing and local area commitment.

At its center, engaging private ventures isn't just about tending to explicit difficulties yet in addition about sustaining a mentality of strength and flexibility. It's tied in with empowering these organizations to embrace change and transform it into an open door as opposed to a danger. By imparting a pioneering soul and a development mentality, we get ready independent ventures for the difficulties of tomorrow.

The effect of engaging independent ventures stretches out a long ways past their singular achievement. It swells through the economy, making an outpouring of advantages. At the point when independent ventures flourish, they enlist more workers, driving down joblessness rates and supporting nearby economies. Their prosperity powers advancement, prompting the improvement of new items and administrations, and drives monetary development. Enabled independent companies are fundamental mainstays of financial versatility, guaranteeing that networks and countries can climate monetary tempests with more noteworthy strength and nimbleness.

Strengthening of independent companies is likewise a useful asset for tending to social and financial differences. It tends to be a way to inspire underserved networks and overcome any issues among metropolitan and country regions. By putting resources into private ventures in these districts, we can animate financial turn of events, lessen destitution, and work on the general personal satisfaction for occupants.

In a quickly changing worldwide scene, the idea of strengthening isn't static. It advances in light of arising difficulties and open doors. As new innovations, financial patterns, and social changes keep on reshaping the business climate, the procedures for enabling independent companies should adjust appropriately.

One of the critical drivers of private company strengthening as of late has been the computerized change. The approach of the web and online business has opened up new roads for private ventures to arrive at a worldwide client base. The democratization of web based showcasing and deals stages has empowered even the littlest ventures to contend on a level battleground with a lot bigger contenders. Advanced devices have additionally smoothed out activities, making it more straightforward for private companies to deal with their funds, interface with clients, and remain cutthroat.

Moreover, the rise of the gig economy has set out open doors for independent ventures to access on-request ability and grow their labor force without the conventional expenses related with recruiting full-time representatives. This adaptability permits private ventures to scale their activities on a case by case basis and adjust to changing economic situations without focusing on long haul commitments.

Maintainability is one more developing component of private venture strengthening. Shoppers and financial backers are progressively focusing on naturally mindful practices and moral business direct. Private ventures that embrace maintainability add to a better planet as well as draw in a developing client base that esteems these standards. Enabling private companies for supportability includes giving them assets, direction, and motivators to take on eco-accommodating practices and incorporate manageability into their plans of action.

Government approaches and guidelines likewise develop as new difficulties emerge. Directly following the Coronavirus pandemic, for instance, numerous states presented alleviation programs and monetary help to assist private companies with enduring the financial tempest. These actions showed the versatility of independent venture strengthening

1.1 Defining the Importance of Small Businesses

Private companies, frequently depicted as the backbone of the worldwide economy, hold an unmistakable and indispensable job in forming the financial and social scenes of countries. These undertakings are the exemplification of enterprising soul and advancement, driving monetary development, work creation, and neighborhood improvement. As we dive into the significance of private ventures, we uncover the horde manners by which they influence networks and economies, and their remarkable characteristics that recognize them from their bigger partners.

The meaning of private companies lies in their strength, versatility, and steady obligation to neighborhood networks. At the point when we discuss independent ventures, we regularly allude to undertakings with less than 500 workers, however many are far more modest, frequently including sole owners and miniature organizations with simply a small bunch of representatives or even a solitary sole proprietor. It is this very unobtrusiveness in size that empowers them to be deft, responsive, and imaginative.

One of the main qualities of independent companies is their ability to act as the foundation of neighborhood economies. They lay out an immediate association among organizations and the networks they work in. Private ventures are much of the time established in their regions, both topographically and socially. They make a feeling of local area, offer customized types of assistance, and proposition remarkable items that take care of the particular requirements and inclinations of their customer base.

Work creation is one of the essential commitments of private ventures to economies all over the planet. They are eminent for their job in producing business potential open doors, especially at the neighborhood level. Whether it's the corner store, the local café, or the shop, private ventures utilize a large number of individuals and, much of the time, extend to the principal employment opportunity experience for some people. The positions they make frequently include many jobs, from cutting edge administration positions to administrative jobs, adding to a different and dynamic labor force.

Besides, private ventures have a penchant to drive financial development through advancement and business. The deftness intrinsic to their little size permits them to rapidly distinguish open doors and adjust to changing economic situations. They frequently act as cauldrons for novel thoughts, inventive critical thinking, and out-of-the-case thinking. In doing as such, they add to mechanical progressions and encourage a culture of business venture.

Private companies are at the front of neighborhood advancement. They support associations with other neighborhood organizations, providers, and clients, shaping an intricate trap of financial and social interdependencies. This interconnectivity reinforces networks by supporting financial versatility. Therefore, independent ventures are in many cases fundamental parts of practical, confident neighborhood economies.

While independent ventures hold remarkable benefits, they likewise face a large group of difficulties and hindrances. Maybe the most inescapable and quick is the question of funding. Admittance to capital is an enduring worry for entrepreneurs. Conventional monetary establishments, like banks, frequently see private ventures as less secure speculations, prompting difficulties in getting advances or credit. This absence of admittance to capital can altogether prevent their development and extension potential.

In a quickly developing mechanical scene, private ventures face another impressive test: staying aware of computerized change. The advanced insurgency has significantly adjusted the manner in which organizations work, from web based business and web based advertising to information examination and computerization. Private ventures might find it challenging to put resources into and adjust to the most recent innovations, given their restricted spending plans and at times lacking mastery.

Also, private companies frequently wrestle with the intricacies of exploring administrative conditions and regulatory formality. The labyrinth of consistence prerequisites, licenses, allows, and expenses can be overpowering for proprietors who as of now wear different caps. These regulatory difficulties can consume significant time and assets, redirecting their consideration from developing and extending their undertakings.

Another test private ventures stand up to is the inescapability of huge organizations. These corporate monsters frequently use gigantic market power, which can prompt uncalled for rivalry and a lopsided battleground. Private companies should fight with the benefits that accompany the scale, assets, and showcasing clout of their bigger rivals.

Perceiving the gravity of these difficulties and the worth independent companies bring to society, the idea of engaging private ventures becomes the dominant focal point. Strengthening connotes the most common way of furnishing private ventures with the devices, assets, and backing important to beat these deterrents and secure their position later on business scene. It includes diverse aspects pointed toward supporting the development, supportability, and strength of private companies.

One pivotal element of private venture strengthening is upgraded admittance to monetary assets. By guaranteeing that private ventures can get the fundamental capital for development and advancement, we address quite possibly of their most critical obstruction. This incorporates customary bank advances as well as elective supporting choices like funding, crowdfunding, and microloans. The enhancement of monetary assets mitigates the dangers related with depending entirely on customary financial channels.

Innovative strengthening is another basic perspective. In the present computerized time, private companies should outfit the force of innovation to stay cutthroat. This includes procuring the most recent instruments and programming as well as acquiring the information and abilities to actually utilize them. Engaging independent ventures with the abilities to explore the advanced scene guarantees they can fulfill the needs of the cutting edge commercial center.

Improvement and smoothing out of guidelines assume a fundamental part in strengthening. States and administrative bodies should attempt to decrease the managerial weight on private ventures, making consistence more direct and productive. The objective is to empower private companies to zero in on their center exercises and development methodologies as opposed to wrestling with extreme administrative work and regulatory intricacies.

Similarly essential is tending to the variations in market power between private companies and bigger partnerships. Strengthening in such manner includes approaches that advance fair rivalry, safeguard against monopolistic practices, and set out open doors for private ventures to team up and frame collusions that help their seriousness. A fair commercial center guarantees that all players, paying little mind to estimate, have an equivalent shot at progress.

Building a strong environment of help is one more fundamental feature of strengthening. Entrepreneurs can benefit incredibly from business warning administrations, mentorship programs, and systems administration open doors. Interfacing them with experienced guides and companions takes into consideration information sharing, best practice trade, and common help, adding to a culture of learning and development.

Past the functional perspectives, encouraging a steady and comprehensive business climate is of fundamental significance. This involves perceiving the remarkable commitments of private ventures and recognizing their part in nearby and worldwide economies. By advancing mindfulness and enthusiasm for private ventures, we can energize buyer support, local area commitment, and a better business environment.

The effect of enabling private ventures stretches out a long ways past their nearby achievement. It resonates all through the economy, making a chain response of advantages. At the point when private ventures prosper, they enlist more workers, adding to decreased joblessness rates and more grounded neighborhood economies. Their prosperity additionally powers advancement, prompting the improvement of new items and administrations, and at last impelling monetary development. Engaged independent companies are fundamental mainstays of financial flexibility, guaranteeing that networks and countries can climate monetary tempests with more noteworthy strength and versatility.

Independent company strengthening is a powerful instrument for tending to social and financial differences. It tends to be utilized to elevate underserved networks, overcome any issues among metropolitan and rustic regions, and invigorate financial turn of events. By putting resources into private companies in these districts, we can decrease destitution, work on the general personal satisfaction for occupants, and set out additional impartial open doors for all.

In a powerful worldwide scene, the idea of strengthening isn't static; it develops because of arising difficulties and potential open doors. For example, the computerized change has essentially modified the independent company strengthening scene. The web and web based business have opened up new roads for independent ventures to arrive at a worldwide client base. Internet showcasing and deals stages have made everything fair, permitting even the littlest undertakings to rival a lot bigger contenders. Advanced devices have smoothed out tasks, making it simpler for private companies to deal with their funds, associate with clients, and remain serious in an undeniably computerized commercial center.

The rise of the gig economy is one more huge advancement in private company strengthening. This new work market model has set out open doors for independent companies to access on-request ability and extend their labor force without the conventional expenses and responsibilities related with recruiting full-time representatives. This adaptability permits private ventures to scale their activities on a case by case basis and adjust to changing economic situations without causing long haul commitments.

Maintainability is one more advancing element of independent company strengthening. With customers and financial backers progressively focusing on ecologically mindful practices and moral business direct, private company.

1.2 The Role of Small Businesses in Local Economies

Private ventures are the soul of neighborhood economies. They are the corner stores, family cafés, shops, and specialist co-ops that shape the personality of neighborhoods and towns across the world. These endeavors assume a key part in cultivating financial development, work creation, and local area improvement. As we investigate the diverse and basic job of private ventures in nearby economies, we reveal the profundity of their effect and the remarkable worth they offer that might be of some value.

Independent companies are regularly characterized as endeavors with less than 500 representatives, yet many are a lot more modest, going from sole ownerships to miniature organizations with just a small bunch of workers. This unobtrusive scale is one of their characterizing highlights, making them light-footed and receptive to the particular requirements of their networks. Private companies are many times established in the neighborhoods they serve, making major areas of strength for an of association among organizations and individuals they take care of.

Work creation stands apart as one of the most quick and critical commitments of independent ventures to nearby economies. They are eminent for creating business potential open doors, frequently at the grassroots level. Whether it's the nearby bistro, the mother and-pop supermarket, or the family-possessed auto mechanics shop, independent companies utilize a different labor force, going from passage level situations to administrative jobs. Their part in giving open positions, particularly for youth and those entering the labor force, couldn't possibly be more significant.

Past work creation, private ventures add to financial development through their inventive soul and versatility. The actual idea of these organizations makes them agile, permitting them to distinguish open doors rapidly and answer changing economic situations. They act as hatcheries for novel thoughts, effective fixes, and whimsical reasoning. In doing as such, they add to mechanical progressions and support a culture of business venture, which meaningfully affects the more extensive economy.

Also, independent companies are personally associated with nearby turn of events. They lay out and keep up with associations with other neighborhood organizations, providers, and clients, shaping a mind boggling trap of monetary and social interdependencies. These interconnections assist with reinforcing networks by upgrading financial versatility. Generally, private ventures are imperative parts of economical and confident neighborhood economies, adding to the development and prosperity of the locales they work in.

Private ventures are likewise prominent for their capacity to cultivate a feeling of local area and restricted economies. Dissimilar to huge, worldwide enterprises, private ventures frequently have a characteristic association with the local area they serve. Proprietors live nearby, and they are known by name to their clients. These organizations give a degree of customized administration and comprehension of nearby inclinations that bigger chains frequently can't coordinate. They add to a feeling of spot and character, making the local area more lively and special.

Be that as it may, private ventures are not without their difficulties. Funding is a critical worry, as admittance to capital can be restricted. Customary monetary foundations, like banks, frequently see private companies as more hazardous speculations, making it trying to get advances or credit. This absence of admittance to capital can prevent the development and extension capability of independent ventures.

In a quickly developing mechanical scene, private companies likewise battle to stay aware of computerized change. The advanced upheaval has impacted the manner in which organizations work, from web based business and web based advertising to information examination and mechanization. Private ventures might find it challenging to put resources into and adjust to the most recent advances because of their restricted spending plans and ability. Subsequently, they can confront a serious disservice in the computerized commercial center.

Additionally, exploring administrative conditions and regulatory cycles can be an overwhelming errand for private ventures. Consistence necessities, licenses, allows, and burdens frequently present managerial difficulties that can consume important time and assets. Proprietors should shuffle numerous obligations, including administrative consistence, which can redirect their consideration from business development and extension.

Private ventures additionally battle with the cutthroat could of huge partnerships. These corporate goliaths use impressive market power, which can prompt unreasonable rivalry and a lopsided battleground. Independent ventures should wrestle with the benefits that accompany the scale, assets, and promoting clout of their bigger rivals.

Perceiving the difficulties that private ventures face and the worth they bring to neighborhood economies, the idea of enabling independent companies takes on a focal job. Strengthening envelops different aspects pointed toward supporting the development, manageability, and flexibility of private ventures in neighborhood economies.

One of the most basic elements of independent venture strengthening is improving their admittance to monetary assets. By guaranteeing that private companies can get the important capital for development and advancement, we address quite possibly of their most critical hindrance. This includes conventional bank advances as well as elective supporting choices like investment, crowdfunding, and microloans. Expanding the wellsprings of monetary help mitigates the dangers related with depending exclusively on regular financial channels.

Mechanical strengthening is similarly crucial. In the advanced age, private companies should tackle the force of innovation to stay cutthroat. This includes getting the most recent instruments and programming as well as acquiring the information and abilities to actually utilize them. Engaging private ventures with the capacities to explore the computerized scene guarantees they can satisfy the needs of the cutting edge commercial center.

One more key component of strengthening is the improvement and smoothing out of guidelines. States and administrative bodies should attempt to lessen the regulatory weight on private companies, making consistence more clear and proficient. The objective is to empower independent ventures to zero in on their center exercises and development systems as opposed to wrestling with extreme desk work and administrative intricacies.

Strengthening likewise includes tending to the differences in market power between private companies and bigger partnerships. Approaches that advance fair contest, safeguard against monopolistic practices, and set out open doors for independent ventures to team up and shape unions can assist with evening the odds. A fair commercial center guarantees that all players, paying little mind to measure, have an equivalent shot at progress.

Besides, building a powerful biological system of help is a fundamental feature of strengthening. Entrepreneurs can benefit incredibly from business warning administrations, mentorship programs, and systems administration amazing open doors. Interfacing them with experienced coaches and companions considers information sharing, best practice trade, and common help, adding to a culture of learning and development.

Encouraging a strong and comprehensive business climate is one more basic component of strengthening. This involves perceiving the novel commitments of private companies and recognizing their part in neighborhood and worldwide economies. By advancing mindfulness and enthusiasm for private ventures, we can empower shopper support, local area commitment, and a better business environment.

The effect of engaging private ventures stretches out a long ways past their nearby achievement. It resounds all through neighborhood economies, making a chain response of advantages. At the point when independent companies flourish, they recruit more workers, diminishing joblessness rates and reinforcing nearby economies.

Their prosperity likewise powers advancement, prompting the improvement of new items and administrations and eventually pushing monetary development. Enabled independent companies are fundamental mainstays of monetary flexibility, guaranteeing that networks and locales can climate financial tempests with more prominent strength and versatility.

Independent venture strengthening is likewise a powerful instrument for tending to social and monetary inconsistencies. It can elevate underserved networks, overcome any issues among metropolitan and country regions, and invigorate financial turn of events. By putting resources into private ventures in these areas, we can decrease destitution, work on the general personal satisfaction for occupants, and set out additional evenhanded open doors for all.

In a quickly changing worldwide scene, the idea of strengthening isn't static. It advances in light of arising difficulties and open doors. The advanced change, for example, has essentially modified the private venture strengthening scene. The web and online business have opened up new roads for independent ventures to arrive at a worldwide client base. Web based advertising and deals stages have made everything fair, permitting even the littlest undertakings to rival a lot bigger contenders. Advanced apparatuses have smoothed out tasks, making it simpler for private ventures to deal with their funds, associate with clients, and remain cutthroat in an undeniably computerized commercial center.

The rise of the gig economy is one more critical improvement in private company strengthening. This new work market model has set out open doors for private ventures to access on-request ability and grow their labor force without the conventional expenses and responsibilities related with recruiting full-time representatives. This adaptability permits private companies to scale their tasks on a case by case basis and adjust to changing economic situations without causing long haul commitments.

Supportability is one more advancing element of independent company strengthening. With purchasers and financial backers progressively focusing on ecologically mindful practices and moral business direct, independent companies that embrace supportability not just add to a health.

1.3 The Relevance of Empowering Small Businesses

Engaging private ventures isn't simply a financial objective; it is a basic need for building strong, comprehensive, and dynamic networks and economies. Private ventures, frequently characterized as those with less than 500 workers, address the foundation of neighborhood and worldwide economies. They contribute essentially to work creation, advancement, and local area improvement. In this conversation, we dig into the significance of engaging private companies, analyzing the bunch manners by which it shapes the future business scene and improves the prosperity of society overall.

Private companies have a few separating characteristics that put them aside and make them especially pertinent in the present monetary and social setting. Their unassuming size and restricted presence empower them to interface with their networks at a more profound level than bigger companies. These organizations are in many cases established in the neighborhoods they serve, encouraging a feeling of trust and individual cooperation with their clients. This limited methodology is critical for building solid networks and encouraging financial versatility.

One of the most prompt and fundamental commitments of independent companies is work creation. They act as imperative wellsprings of business, especially at the neighborhood level. These organizations frequently enlist people from the local area, extending to an extensive variety of open positions, from section level situations to administrative jobs. Thus, private ventures assume a vital part in lessening joblessness rates and giving work to youth and those entering the labor force.

Private companies additionally drive monetary development through their imaginative soul and flexibility. Their limited scale makes them lithe and responsive, empowering them to jump all over chances and adjust to changing economic situations rapidly. They frequently act as hatcheries for groundbreaking thoughts, inventive critical thinking, and out-of-the-container thinking. This culture of development cultivates enterprising soul as well as prompts mechanical headways that benefit the more extensive economy.

Besides, the associations that independent companies lay out with other nearby substances, including providers, clients, and adjoining organizations, make a trap of monetary and social interdependencies. This organization reinforces networks by upgrading financial versatility, guaranteeing that nearby economies can endure monetary shocks and difficulties. Independent ventures are key supporters of confident, maintainable nearby economies.

Notwithstanding their financial commitments, private ventures are imperative for encouraging a feeling of local area and character. Not at all like enormous, worldwide companies, private ventures have an inborn association with the local area they serve. Proprietors frequently live in similar areas as their organizations and are known by name to their clients. They offer customized types of assistance and grasp the particular requirements and inclinations of their customer base, adding to a special feeling of spot and neighborhood personality.

Notwithstanding their irrefutable significance, independent companies face various difficulties that can obstruct their development and manageability. Funding stays an unmistakable issue, as admittance to capital is many times restricted. Conventional monetary foundations might see private ventures as more dangerous speculations, making it challenging for these organizations to get advances or credit. This absence of admittance to capital can essentially impede their extension and advancement potential.

Also, independent companies frequently battle to stay up with the computerized change. The advanced insurgency has reshaped business tasks, from web based business and internet advertising to information investigation and computerization. Private companies might find it trying to put resources into and adjust to the most recent innovations because of their restricted spending plans and, on occasion, an absence of skill. This computerized hole can prompt a serious detriment in the cutting edge commercial center.

Administrative obstacles and administrative intricacies additionally present difficulties for private ventures. Consistence necessities, licenses, allows, and burdens frequently consume a lot of time and assets. Entrepreneurs are compelled to shuffle numerous obligations, including administrative consistence, which can diminish their essential spotlight on business development and extension.

Besides, private ventures frequently wind up in direct contest with huge partnerships, which have critical market power. The scale, assets, and advertising abilities of these corporate goliaths can make a lopsided battleground, making it hard for independent companies to contend. Unreasonable rivalry can smother the development and flourishing of little undertakings.

Perceiving the meaning of independent companies and the obstructions they face, the idea of enabling them becomes the dominant focal point. Strengthening alludes to the most common way of furnishing private companies with the apparatuses, assets, and backing expected to defeat these difficulties and secure their spot later on business scene. Strengthening incorporates different aspects pointed toward reinforcing the development, maintainability, and versatility of independent companies.

One of the most basic components of independent venture strengthening is improving their admittance to monetary assets. By guaranteeing that independent ventures can get the essential capital for development and advancement, one of their most critical hindrances is tended to. This includes customary bank advances as well as elective funding choices like investment, crowdfunding, and microloans. Expanding the wellsprings of monetary help mitigates the dangers related with depending exclusively on ordinary financial channels.

Innovative strengthening is another basic viewpoint. In the present computerized age, private companies should bridle the force of innovation to stay cutthroat. This includes getting the most recent devices and programming as well as acquiring the information and abilities to successfully utilize them. Enabling private companies with the capacities to explore the computerized scene guarantees they can satisfy the needs of the advanced commercial center.

Disentanglement and smoothing out of guidelines assume a critical part in strengthening. States and administrative bodies should attempt to decrease the regulatory weight on independent ventures, making consistence more direct and proficient.

The objective is to empower independent ventures to zero in on their center exercises and development procedures as opposed to wrestling with unreasonable desk work and administrative intricacies.

Tending to the variations in market power between private companies and bigger organizations is a critical part of strengthening. Arrangements that advance fair contest, safeguard against monopolistic practices, and set out open doors for independent companies to team up and frame unions can even the odds. A fair commercial center guarantees that all players, paying little mind to measure, have an equivalent shot at progress.

Building a strong biological system of help is one more fundamental feature of strengthening. Entrepreneurs can benefit enormously from business warning administrations, mentorship programs, and systems administration potential open doors. Interfacing them with experienced guides and friends takes into consideration information sharing, best practice trade, and common help, adding to a culture of learning and development.

Cultivating a strong and comprehensive business climate is likewise of fundamental significance. This involves perceiving the novel commitments of private ventures and recognizing their job in neighborhood and worldwide economies. By advancing mindfulness and enthusiasm for private ventures, we can energize purchaser support, local area commitment, and a better business environment.

The effect of enabling independent companies reaches out a long ways past their singular achievement. It resonates all through the economy, making a chain response of advantages. At the point when private companies flourish, they enlist more representatives, adding to decreased joblessness rates and more grounded nearby economies. Their prosperity powers advancement, prompting the improvement of new items and administrations, and eventually moving monetary development. Engaged private ventures are fundamental mainstays of monetary versatility, guaranteeing that networks and countries can climate financial tempests with more noteworthy strength and flexibility.

Strengthening of private companies is likewise an integral asset for tending to social and monetary variations. It very well may be a way to elevate underserved networks, overcome any barrier among metropolitan and country regions, and invigorate financial turn of events. By putting resources into private companies in these locales, we can lessen neediness, work on the general personal satisfaction for occupants, and set out additional fair open doors for all.

In a quickly changing worldwide scene, the idea of strengthening isn't static. It develops because of arising difficulties and open doors. For instance, the computerized change has altogether adjusted the private company strengthening scene. The coming of the web and internet business has opened up new roads for private companies to arrive at a worldwide client base.

The democratization of internet promoting and deals stages has empowered even the littlest ventures to contend on a level battleground with a lot bigger contenders. Computerized devices have likewise smoothed out tasks, making it simpler for private ventures to deal with their funds, associate with clients, and remain serious in an undeniably advanced commercial center.

The rise of the gig economy is one more huge advancement in private venture strengthening. This new work market model has set out open doors for independent companies to access on-request ability and extend their labor force without the customary expenses and responsibilities related with recruiting full-time representatives. This adaptability permits private companies to scale their activities depending on the situation and adjust to changing economic situations without bringing about long haul commitments.

Chapter 2

The Economic Impact

The monetary scene is a mind boggling embroidery of different components, and at the core, all things considered, are private companies. These ventures, frequently portrayed by their unobtrusive size and restricted presence, employ a critical impact on economies at neighborhood, public, and, surprisingly, worldwide levels. The financial effect of engaging private companies couldn't possibly be more significant, as they act as impetuses for development, work creation, and advancement. In this investigation, we dive into the significant monetary impact of private ventures and the extraordinary impact of enabling them.

Private ventures, as characterized by having less than 500 representatives, assume a crucial part in forming the monetary scene. Their commitment rises above simple numbers, as their innate attributes make them interestingly ready to drive monetary development, work creation, and advancement. As a matter of fact, these organizations are the foundation of numerous economies, contributing significantly to both Gross domestic product and generally business.

Work creation is one of the most prompt and critical commitments of private companies to economies. They are famous for creating business open doors, especially at the neighborhood level. Private companies frequently recruit people from the local area, giving an extensive variety of open positions, from passage level situations to administrative jobs. Their part in offering work for youth and those entering the labor force can't be overemphasized.

Besides, independent ventures are a power of development and flexibility. Their limited scale and nearby center empower them to be coordinated and receptive to advertise changes. They rapidly recognize open doors, adjust to moving shopper inclinations, and investigation with effective fixes. Private companies act as hotbeds for enterprising soul and creative reasoning, adding to mechanical progressions and encouraging a culture of business.

Past work creation and advancement, private ventures are profoundly imbued in neighborhood improvement. They lay out and keep up with associations with other nearby substances, including providers, clients, and adjoining organizations, making a snare of monetary and social interdependencies. These interconnections improve financial versatility, adding to confident and feasible nearby economies.

Private companies likewise encourage a feeling of local area and spot. Dissimilar to huge, global enterprises, private ventures have an inborn association with the networks they serve. Proprietors frequently live in similar areas as their organizations and are known by name to their clients. They offer customized types of assistance and grasp the particular necessities and inclinations of their customer base, adding to a novel feeling of nearby personality.

In any case, private ventures are not safe to challenges. Regardless of their critical job in the monetary scene, they frequently face deterrents that can frustrate their development and maintainability. Admittance to capital is a conspicuous issue, as customary monetary organizations might see private ventures as less secure speculations. This discernment makes it challenging for private ventures to get advances or credit, restricting their development and advancement potential.

The advanced change presents one more considerable test for private companies. In the quickly developing mechanical scene, staying aware of the most recent computerized apparatuses and stages is fundamental for seriousness. Nonetheless, private ventures might battle to put resources into and adjust to these innovations, given their restricted spending plans and, on occasion, an absence of skill. This computerized gap can bring about a cutthroat hindrance.

Administrative obstacles and administrative intricacies additionally present hardships for independent ventures. Consistence prerequisites, licenses, allows, and burdens frequently request huge time and assets. Entrepreneurs, currently troubled with different obligations, end up shuffling administrative consistence close by center business exercises, taking away from their development potential.

Moreover, the serious force of enormous organizations can make a lopsided battleground for independent ventures. Corporate goliaths have tremendous assets, market impact, and promoting abilities that can make it trying for independent companies to contend. Uncalled for rivalry can thwart the development and thriving of little undertakings.

Perceiving the difficulties that private companies face and their irrefutable monetary commitments, the idea of enabling them becomes fundamental. Strengthening includes outfitting private ventures with the devices, assets, and backing expected to defeat these difficulties and secure their spot in the financial scene. Strengthening includes different aspects pointed toward reinforcing the development, manageability, and versatility of independent ventures.

One of the most basic elements of private company strengthening is upgrading their admittance to monetary assets. By guaranteeing that independent ventures can get the vital capital for development and advancement, one of their most critical obstructions is tended to. This includes conventional bank advances as well as elective funding choices like investment, crowdfunding, and microloans. Broadening the well-springs of monetary help mitigates the dangers related with depending entirely on regular financial channels.

Innovative strengthening is one more principal part of engaging private ventures. In the advanced age, private ventures should saddle the force of innovation to stay cutthroat. This includes getting the most recent apparatuses and programming as well as acquiring the information and abilities to successfully utilize them. Engaging private ventures with the abilities to explore the computerized scene guarantees they can satisfy the needs of the advanced commercial center.

Disentanglement and smoothing out of guidelines assume a significant part in strengthening. Legislatures and administrative bodies should attempt to diminish the authoritative weight on private ventures, making consistence more direct and productive. The objective is to empower private ventures to zero in on their center exercises and development methodologies as opposed to wrestling with unnecessary desk work and regulatory intricacies.

Tending to the variations in market power between private ventures and bigger organizations is a vital part of strengthening. Approaches that advance fair contest, safeguard against monopolistic practices, and set out open doors for independent ventures to team up and shape partnerships can even the odds. A decent commercial center guarantees that all players, paying little mind to measure, have an equivalent shot at progress.

Building a strong environment of help is one more fundamental feature of strengthening. Entrepreneurs can benefit extraordinarily from business warning administrations, mentorship programs, and systems administration open doors. Interfacing them with experienced coaches and friends considers information sharing, best practice trade, and common help, adding to a culture of learning and development.

Encouraging a steady and comprehensive business climate is likewise of foremost significance. This involves perceiving the exceptional commitments of private ventures and recognizing their part in nearby and worldwide economies. By advancing mindfulness and enthusiasm for independent ventures, we can energize buyer support, local area commitment, and a better business environment.

The effect of enabling independent ventures reaches out a long ways past their singular achievement. It resonates all through the economy, making a chain response of advantages. At the point when private companies flourish, they enlist more representatives, adding to diminished joblessness rates and more grounded nearby economies.

Their prosperity powers advancement, prompting the improvement of new items and administrations, and at last pushing financial development. Enabled private ventures are fundamental mainstays of monetary flexibility, guaranteeing that networks and countries can climate financial tempests with more noteworthy strength and versatility.

Besides, independent company strengthening is a strong device for tending to social and monetary variations. It can inspire underserved networks, overcome any issues among metropolitan and provincial regions, and animate monetary turn of events. By putting resources into private ventures in these areas, we can diminish destitution, work on the general personal satisfaction for occupants, and set out additional even-handed open doors for all.

In a quickly changing worldwide scene, the idea of strengthening isn't static. It develops in light of arising difficulties and open doors. The computerized change has essentially modified the private company strengthening scene. The web and internet business have opened up new roads for independent companies to arrive at a worldwide client base. Internet promoting and deals stages have made everything fair, permitting even the littlest undertakings to rival a lot bigger contenders. Computerized devices have smoothed out activities, making it simpler for private companies to deal with their funds, associate with clients, and remain cutthroat in an undeniably advanced commercial center.

The rise of the gig economy is one more huge improvement in private venture strengthening. This new work market model has set out open doors for independent companies to access on-request ability and grow their labor force without the customary expenses and responsibilities related with recruiting full-time representatives. This adaptability permits independent companies to scale their activities depending on the situation and adjust to changing economic situations without bringing about long haul commitments.

Manageability is one more advancing component of private venture strengthening. With shoppers and financial backers progressively focusing on ecologically dependable practices and moral business lead, independent companies that embrace supportability add to a better planet as well as draw in a developing client base that esteems these standards. Engaging independent companies for manageability includes giving them .

2.1 Small Businesses as Engines of Economic Growth

Independent ventures, frequently characterized by their unobtrusive size and limited presence, act as motors of monetary development. These ventures are essential to the financial texture of networks, countries, and the worldwide economy. Their novel attributes, including position creation, advancement, and versatility, make them crucial supporters of financial turn of events. In this investigation, we dive into the multi-layered job of private companies as drivers of financial development and the extraordinary impact of engaging them.

Independent ventures are regularly classified by having less than 500 workers. While this order might seem inconsistent, it addresses a wide range of undertakings, from sole ownerships and privately-run companies to new businesses and creative endeavors. In spite of their variety, private companies share normal attributes that recognize them as motors of monetary development.

One of the most prompt and huge commitments of independent companies to financial development is work creation. These endeavors are famous for creating business open doors, especially at the nearby level. Independent companies frequently act as fundamental causes of employment opportunities, giving an extensive variety of business prospects, from section level situations to administrative jobs. Their capacity to enlist people from the local area, including youth and those entering the labor force, is pivotal for lessening joblessness rates and cultivating monetary turn of events.

Besides, private companies assume a crucial part in driving monetary development through their imaginative soul and versatility. Their limited scale permits them to be deft and receptive to changing economic situations. They rapidly distinguish open doors, answer moving buyer inclinations, and examination with intelligent fixes. Independent ventures act as hatcheries for novel thoughts, innovative critical thinking, and out-of-the-crate thinking. This culture of development encourages innovative soul as well as prompts mechanical progressions that benefit the more extensive economy.

Past work creation and advancement, independent ventures are profoundly interconnected with nearby turn of events. They lay out and keep up with associations with other nearby substances, including providers, clients, and adjoining organizations, making a trap of financial and social interdependencies. These interconnections upgrade monetary flexibility, adding to independent and manageable nearby economies.

Independent ventures likewise encourage a feeling of local area and personality. Dissimilar to huge, global enterprises, independent ventures have a characteristic association with the networks they serve. Proprietors frequently live in similar areas as their organizations and are known by name to their clients. They offer customized types of assistance and figure out the particular necessities and inclinations of their customer base, adding to an exceptional feeling of spot and neighborhood character.

In spite of their certain significance, private ventures face different difficulties that can impede their development and manageability. Admittance to capital is an unmistakable issue, as conventional monetary foundations might see independent ventures as less secure speculations. This insight makes it hard for independent ventures to get advances or credit, restricting their development and advancement potential.

In the computerized age, private ventures frequently battle to stay up with the advanced change. The fast development of innovation has reshaped business activities, from web based business and internet showcasing to information examination and robotization. Private ventures might find it trying to put resources into and adjust to the most recent innovations because of their restricted spending plans and, on occasion, an absence of skill. This computerized hole can bring about a serious disservice in the cutting edge commercial center.

Administrative obstacles and administrative intricacies likewise present hardships for independent companies. Consistence prerequisites, licenses, allows, and burdens frequently request critical time and assets. Entrepreneurs, currently troubled with various obligations, wind up shuffling administrative consistence close by center business exercises, diminishing their development potential.

Besides, private companies frequently end up in direct contest with enormous enterprises, which have significant market power. Corporate goliaths employ tremendous assets, market impact, and advertising abilities that can make it trying for private companies to contend. Unreasonable rivalry can block the development and flourishing of little ventures.

Perceiving the difficulties that independent ventures face and their certain financial commitments, the idea of enabling them becomes fundamental. Strengthening includes outfitting private ventures with the apparatuses, assets, and backing expected to defeat these difficulties and secure their position in the monetary scene. Strengthening incorporates different aspects pointed toward fortifying the development, manageability, and flexibility of private ventures.

One of the most basic elements of independent venture strengthening is upgrading their admittance to monetary assets. By guaranteeing that independent companies can get the fundamental capital for development and advancement, one of their most critical hindrances is tended to. This includes conventional bank advances as well as elective supporting choices like investment, crowdfunding, and microloans. Differentiating the wellsprings of monetary help mitigates the dangers related with depending entirely on traditional financial channels.

Innovative strengthening is one more essential part of engaging independent ventures. In the advanced age, private companies should bridle the force of innovation to stay serious. This includes getting the most recent apparatuses and programming as well as acquiring the information and abilities to actually utilize them. Engaging independent companies with the abilities to explore the computerized scene guarantees they can fulfill the needs of the advanced commercial center.

Disentanglement and smoothing out of guidelines assume a urgent part in strengthening. Legislatures and administrative bodies should attempt to decrease the regulatory weight on independent ventures, making consistence more clear and productive.

The objective is to empower independent companies to zero in on their center exercises and development techniques as opposed to wrestling with exorbitant desk work and regulatory intricacies.

Tending to the differences in market power between private ventures and bigger enterprises is a significant part of strengthening. Arrangements that advance fair rivalry, safeguard against monopolistic practices, and set out open doors for private companies to team up and shape partnerships can even the odds. A fair commercial center guarantees that all players, paying little mind to estimate, have an equivalent shot at progress.

Building a hearty environment of help is one more fundamental feature of strengthening. Entrepreneurs can benefit enormously from business warning administrations, mentorship programs, and systems administration open doors. Interfacing them with experienced coaches and friends takes into consideration information sharing, best practice trade, and common help, adding to a culture of learning and development.

Encouraging a strong and comprehensive business climate is likewise of foremost significance. This involves perceiving the novel commitments of private ventures and recognizing their job in nearby and worldwide economies. By advancing mindfulness and enthusiasm for private companies, we can energize customer support, local area commitment, and a better business environment.

The effect of enabling private companies stretches out a long ways past their singular achievement. It resonates all through the economy, making a chain response of advantages. At the point when private companies flourish, they recruit more workers, adding to diminished joblessness rates and more grounded nearby economies. Their prosperity energizes advancement, prompting the improvement of new items and administrations, and at last pushing monetary development. Engaged independent companies are fundamental mainstays of financial versatility, guaranteeing that networks and countries can climate monetary tempests with more prominent strength and flexibility.

Independent company strengthening is likewise a powerful device for tending to social and monetary inconsistencies. It can inspire underserved networks, overcome any barrier among metropolitan and country regions, and animate monetary turn of events. By putting resources into private companies in these areas, we can diminish neediness, work on the general personal satisfaction for occupants, and set out additional evenhanded open doors for all.

In a quickly changing worldwide scene, the idea of strengthening isn't static. It develops in light of arising difficulties and open doors. The computerized change has essentially adjusted the independent venture strengthening scene. The coming of the web and online business has opened up new roads for private companies to arrive at a worldwide client base. The democratization of internet showcasing and deals stages has empowered even the littlest ventures to contend on a level battleground with a lot bigger contenders.

Computerized apparatuses have likewise smoothed out activities, making it more straightforward for private companies to deal with their funds, associate with clients, and remain cutthroat in an undeniably advanced commercial center.

The rise of the gig economy is one more huge improvement in private venture strengthening. This new work market model has set out open doors for independent companies to access on-request ability and grow their labor force without the customary expenses and responsibilities related with recruiting full-time representatives. This adaptability permits private companies to scale their tasks depending on the situation and adjust to changing economic situations without causing long haul commitments.

2.2 Job Creation and Employment Opportunities

Private ventures are in many cases proclaimed as the motors of occupation creation, with their huge commitments to business open doors assuming a crucial part in forming the financial scene. These undertakings, portrayed by their unobtrusive size and confined presence, act as fundamental causes of employment opportunities, especially at the nearby level. In this investigation, we dig into the multi-layered job of private companies in producing work open doors, their significance in diminishing joblessness rates, and the groundbreaking impact of enabling them.

Private ventures, typically characterized as those with less than 500 workers, are prestigious for their capacity to make occupations. They act as vital wellsprings of work open doors, especially at the nearby level. Entrepreneurs frequently employ people from the local area, giving an extensive variety of occupation prospects, from section level situations to administrative jobs. This confined way to deal with work creation is instrumental in diminishing joblessness rates and encouraging financial turn of events.

The effect of private ventures on work is significant. As indicated by information from the U.S. Private venture Organization (SBA), private ventures were liable for making 1.6 million net positions in 2019. This figure highlights the meaning of these ventures as occupation generators. The capacity of independent ventures to extend to different open positions, customized to the requirements of their networks, adds to the financial advancement of districts and cultivates monetary versatility.

Besides, independent ventures can possibly act as hatcheries for business. They set out open doors for trying business people, work searchers, and people looking for vocation development. By offering business and expert turn of events, independent ventures assist with molding the labor force and cultivate the abilities and skill fundamental for more extensive monetary achievement.

The significance of private ventures in diminishing joblessness rates can't be put into words. These endeavors give a critical number of occupations as well as target different portions of the labor force, including late alumni, people looking for vocation changes, and those reemerging the work market. This inclusivity in their employing rehearses decreases joblessness rates and achieves a more adjusted and dynamic labor force.

Moreover, independent companies frequently focus on nearby recruiting, adding to the financial advancement of their networks. They effectively draw in with occupants, employing people who live in similar areas and figure out the particular requirements and inclinations of their customers. This restricted way to deal with work encourages a feeling of spot and personality, fortifying the social texture of networks.

Enabling private ventures with regards to work creation includes a few aspects. One of the most quick methodologies is to help their development and extension. By furnishing independent ventures with admittance to monetary assets, they can recruit more representatives and proposition more open positions. Strengthening might incorporate different types of supporting, including conventional bank credits, funding, crowdfunding, or microloans, guaranteeing that independent ventures can get the vital capital for development.

Innovative strengthening is another basic perspective. In the cutting edge computerized age, private companies should saddle the force of innovation to stay cutthroat. This includes obtaining the most recent apparatuses and programming as well as acquiring the information and abilities to successfully utilize them. Enabling independent companies with the abilities to explore the computerized scene guarantees they can fulfill the needs of the advanced commercial center, eventually prompting greater work open doors.

Smoothing out guidelines is one more fundamental element of private company strengthening with regards to work creation. Decreasing the managerial weight on private ventures and making consistence with guidelines more direct and effective can empower them to zero in on their center exercises and development procedures. The objective is to diminish the time and assets spent on administrative consistence, hence opening up limit with regards to growing the labor force.

Tending to differences in market power between private ventures and bigger companies is a crucial part of strengthening. Arrangements that advance fair rivalry, safeguard against monopolistic practices, and set out open doors for independent ventures to team up and frame collusions can even the odds. A reasonable commercial center guarantees that independent companies, no matter what their size, have an equivalent shot at progress, permitting them to set out more work open doors.

Building a strong biological system of help is instrumental in private company strengthening for work creation. Entrepreneurs can benefit enormously from business warning administrations, mentorship programs, and systems administration valuable open doors. Interfacing them with experienced guides and companions takes into consideration information sharing, best practice trade, and common help, at last prompting more successful labor force the executives and occupation creation.

Cultivating a steady and comprehensive business climate is likewise of principal significance with regards to work creation. Perceiving the special commitments of private companies and recognizing their part in neighborhood and worldwide economies can empower purchaser support, local area commitment, and a better business environment. At the point when independent companies feel upheld by their networks and state run administrations, they are bound to grow and set out unexpected work open doors.

The effect of enabling independent companies for work creation stretches out a long ways past the singular level. At the point when private ventures flourish, they enlist more workers, adding to diminished joblessness rates and more grounded nearby economies. The capacity to create business valuable open doors prompts a better personal satisfaction for occupants and cultivates financial turn of events.

Private companies assume a necessary part in cultivating a different and comprehensive labor force. Their confined way to deal with employing gives amazing open doors to people from different foundations and ability levels. This inclusivity upgrades variety in the labor force and adds to a more delegate work market, where everybody has the potential chance to contribute and succeed.

Enabling private companies for work creation isn't exclusively a financial undertaking; it likewise addresses social and monetary variations. Private ventures can elevate underserved networks, overcome any issues among metropolitan and country regions, and animate monetary advancement in districts where open doors are scant. By putting resources into private companies here, we can decrease destitution, work on the general personal satisfaction for occupants, and set out additional fair open doors for all.

In a quickly changing worldwide scene, the idea of strengthening isn't static. It develops in light of arising difficulties and open doors. For instance, the computerized change has essentially modified the private venture strengthening scene. The appearance of the web and online business has opened up new roads for independent ventures to arrive at a worldwide client base. Web based promoting and deals stages have democratized the business climate, permitting even the littlest undertakings to rival a lot bigger contenders. Computerized instruments have smoothed out activities.

2.3 Fostering Innovation in Local Economies

Private ventures, frequently portrayed by their unassuming size and restricted presence, are not only motors of occupation creation; they likewise assume an essential part in driving development inside their networks. These undertakings flourish with versatility, inventiveness, and a nearby association with their clients, making them hotbeds of development. In this investigation, we dig into the multi-layered job of private ventures in cultivating development, their effect on mechanical progressions, and the groundbreaking impact of enabling them to push the limits of imagination.

Private ventures, regularly characterized by having less than 500 representatives, are famous for their capacity to enhance. Their limited scale and restricted center empower them to be spry and receptive to changing economic situations. These undertakings rapidly distinguish amazing open doors, adjust to moving shopper inclinations, and analysis with effective fixes. The actual idea of independent companies supports enterprising soul and out-of-the-container thinking, making them appropriate to driving advancement.

Development inside independent companies reaches out past mechanical progressions; it envelops a more extensive range of savvy fixes, process upgrades, and interesting ways to deal with critical thinking. Entrepreneurs and workers frequently wear different caps, which encourages cross-practical mastery and a different scope of abilities. This variety of thought and experience empowers the advancement of creative thoughts and the execution of unpredictable arrangements.

The limited idea of private companies is a critical driver of development. These ventures lay out and keep up with cozy associations with their networks, clients, and providers. This vicinity and network empower private ventures to have a profound comprehension of nearby requirements and inclinations, permitting them to fit their items and administrations to satisfy explicit needs. This limited way to deal with business tasks frequently prompts the production of inventive, local area driven arrangements.

In addition, private ventures are not hampered by the organization and various leveled structures frequently tracked down in bigger enterprises. This deftness and adaptability permit private ventures to carry out groundbreaking thoughts and trial with intelligent fixes quickly. They can rapidly turn because of changing conditions and market elements, which is a basic part of encouraging development.

Advancement in private ventures isn't restricted to item improvement. These ventures likewise take part in process development, seeing as additional proficient and compelling ways of running their tasks. By ceaselessly looking for upgrades and refining their interior cycles, private companies can improve their efficiency and intensity.

The extraordinary impact of engaging private ventures to cultivate development includes a few aspects. Admittance to monetary assets is fundamental, as it empowers private companies to put resources into innovative work, procure state of the art innovation, and carry out imaginative arrangements. Strengthening incorporates different types of supporting, for example, conventional bank advances, investment, crowdfunding, or microloans, guaranteeing that private companies can tie down the essential funding to fuel their innovative undertakings.

Mechanical strengthening is one more basic part of advancement in private companies. In the advanced computerized age, private companies should outfit the force of innovation to stay cutthroat. This includes obtaining the most recent apparatuses and programming as well as acquiring the information and abilities to really utilize them. Enabling private ventures with the abilities to explore the computerized scene guarantees they can develop because of the requests of the cutting edge commercial center.

Smoothing out guidelines is one more urgent element of private venture strengthening with regards to advancement. Diminishing the managerial weight on private companies and making consistence with guidelines more clear and proficient permits these endeavors to zero in their endeavors on advancement as opposed to wrestling with unnecessary desk work and administrative intricacies.

Tending to differences in market power between private ventures and bigger companies is urgent for cultivating advancement. Arrangements that advance fair rivalry, safeguard against monopolistic practices, and set out open doors for independent companies to team up and frame coalitions can even the odds. A decent commercial center guarantees that private ventures have an equivalent shot at progress, in this manner empowering them to improve.

Building a powerful biological system of help is instrumental in private company strengthening for encouraging development. Entrepreneurs can benefit enormously from business warning administrations, mentorship programs, and systems administration open doors. Associating them with experienced guides and companions takes into consideration information sharing, best practice trade, and common help, at last prompting more creative arrangements.

Cultivating a strong and comprehensive business climate is likewise of central significance with regards to development. Perceiving the one of a kind commitments of private ventures and recognizing their job in nearby and worldwide economies can empower local area commitment, buyer support, and a better business environment. At the point when independent ventures feel upheld by their networks and legislatures, they are bound to improve and add to effective fixes.

The effect of enabling independent ventures for advancement reaches out past the singular level. At the point when independent ventures flourish and develop, they add to innovative progressions, process enhancements, and one of a kind arrangements. This imaginative soul makes a culture of learning and transformation, helping the private company itself as well as impacting the more extensive business environment.

Private companies frequently participate in joint efforts and associations with neighborhood instructive foundations and exploration focuses. These coordinated efforts can prompt information move, research forward leaps, and the advancement of new items or administrations. Enabling private companies to frame such coalitions upgrades their creative capacities and adds to the more extensive information based economy.

Development inside private companies additionally converts into further developed items and administrations that take care of explicit neighborhood needs. These imaginative arrangements can improve the general personal satisfaction for neighborhood occupants and add to local area advancement. Private ventures, well established in their networks, comprehend the special difficulties and potential open doors present, making them strategically set up to make arrangements that address neighborhood issues.

Engaging independent ventures to encourage advancement improves their own seriousness as well as adds to the monetary development and versatility of their networks. Imaginative arrangements frequently bring about the making of new market open doors and the fascination of clients past the neighborhood, supporting monetary turn of events.

In a quickly changing worldwide scene, the idea of strengthening with regards to development isn't static. It advances in light of arising difficulties and potential open doors. For instance, the advanced change has fundamentally modified the independent venture strengthening scene. The approach of the web and web based business has opened up new roads for independent companies to arrive at a worldwide client base. Internet promoting and deals stages have democratized the business climate, permitting even the littlest undertakings to contend on a level battleground with a lot bigger contenders. Computerized apparatuses have smoothed out tasks, making it simpler for private ventures to foster imaginative arrangements and put up them for sale to the public.

The rise of the gig economy is one more critical improvement in private company strengthening for cultivating advancement. This new work market model has set out open doors for independent ventures to access on-request ability and extend their labor force without the customary expenses and responsibilities related with recruiting full-time representatives. Private companies can take advantage of a pool of different abilities and skill, permitting them to participate in greater and specific development endeavors.

Maintainability is one more advancing component of independent venture strengthening for encouraging advancement. With expanding accentuation on ecologically mindful practices and moral business direct, private ventures that embrace manageability add to a better planet as well as draw in a developing client base that esteems these standards. Enabling private companies for maintainability urges them to improve as far as eco-accommodating practices and incorporate supportability into their plans of action.

Government approaches and guidelines likewise adjust in light of new difficulties and open doors in the domain of advancement. For instance, during the Coronavirus pandemic, numerous legislatures presented alleviation programs and monetary help to help private ventures turn and improve in light of the emergency. These actions exhibited the adaptability of private company strengthening methodologies, as states immediately prepared to give fundamental guide during a period of scarcity.

The significance of cultivating advancement in private ventures stretches out a long ways past their singular achievement. It resounds all through the economy, making a chain response of advantages. Inventive independent ventures drive financial development as well as make occupations and add to local area advancement. Their capacity to tackle nearby issues and address explicit issues improves the personal satisfaction for occupants and draws in additional interest nearby.

Chapter 3

Small Businesses and Community

Independent ventures, frequently portrayed by their unobtrusive size and restricted presence, are profoundly entwined with the networks they serve. These endeavors are something beyond monetary substances; they are fundamental parts of the social texture. Private ventures cultivate a feeling of local area, offer customized types of assistance, and make an interesting feeling of spot. In this investigation, we dive into the multi-layered connection between private companies and the networks they occupy, stressing the imperative job these endeavors play in local area improvement and union.

Independent companies, ordinarily characterized as those with less than 500 workers, lay out and keep up with cozy associations with their networks, clients, and providers. This nearness and network empower private companies to have a profound comprehension of nearby requirements and inclinations, permitting them to fit their items and administrations to satisfy explicit needs. This restricted way to deal with business tasks prompts local area driven arrangements as well as cultivates a significant feeling of association and shared help.

Perhaps of the most clear manner by which private companies add to their networks is through work creation. These undertakings are significant wellsprings of business valuable open doors, extending to assorted employment opportunity prospects, from section level situations to administrative jobs. By recruiting people from the local area, private companies diminish joblessness rates as well as construct more grounded social connections among bosses and workers. This limited way to deal with recruiting encourages a feeling of having a place and common perspective, adding to local area improvement and union.

Moreover, independent companies frequently focus on neighborhood employing, which upgrades local area improvement and adds to the financial prosperity of the district. They draw in with occupants, employing people who live in similar areas, grasp the particular requirements and inclinations of their customers, and effectively partake in local area life. This limited way to deal with work encourages a feeling of spot and character, reinforcing the social texture of the local area.

Notwithstanding position creation, private companies likewise participate in generous exercises and local area association. Numerous entrepreneurs live in similar networks where they work their organizations, making them actually put resources into the prosperity of the area. They frequently support nearby occasions, support magnanimous associations, and take part in drives that address local area needs. These commitments go past financial exchanges and mirror a pledge to local area improvement and improvement.

Independent ventures are not simply financial elements; they are fundamental pieces of the social texture. Their limited presence, local area commitment, and customized administrations make a novel feeling of spot and personality. Clients frequently have individual associations with entrepreneurs and representatives, encouraging a sensation of trust, having a place, and shared values. This feeling of association rises above simple exchanges and cultivates a more profound connection between the local area and its private companies.

Engaging private companies to add to local area improvement and attachment includes a few aspects. Admittance to monetary assets is fundamental, as it empowers private ventures to put resources into work creation and local area inclusion. Strengthening incorporates different types of funding, for example, customary bank credits, investment, crowdfunding, or microloans, guaranteeing that independent companies can tie down the important cash-flow to help local area advancement drives.

Smoothing out guidelines is one more pivotal component of private venture strengthening with regards to local area contribution. Diminishing the managerial weight on independent ventures and making consistence with guidelines more clear and effective permits these endeavors to devote additional time and assets to local area drives. The objective is to establish a climate where private ventures can draw in with their networks without extreme regulatory requirements.

Tending to differences in market power between private companies and bigger enterprises is essential for enabling private ventures to assume a functioning part in local area advancement. Arrangements that advance fair rivalry, safeguard against monopolistic practices, and set out open doors for private companies to team up and shape coalitions can even the odds. A decent commercial center guarantees that private ventures have the assets and impact to really draw in with their networks.

Building a hearty environment of help is instrumental in private company strengthening for local area contribution. Entrepreneurs can benefit extraordinarily from business warning administrations, mentorship programs, and systems administration open doors. Associating them with experienced coaches and friends takes into account information sharing, best practice trade, and common help, at last prompting more powerful local area commitment.

Cultivating a strong and comprehensive business climate is likewise of principal significance with regards to local area improvement. Perceiving the exceptional commitments of private ventures and recognizing their part in neighborhood and worldwide economies can empower local area support, shopper commitment, and a better business environment. At the point when private ventures feel upheld by their networks and state run administrations, they are bound to participate in local area improvement drives.

The effect of enabling independent companies to draw in with their networks reaches out a long ways past the singular level. At the point when private companies effectively add to local area improvement, they make a chain response of advantages. These commitments not just upgrade the general personal satisfaction for nearby occupants yet additionally animate financial turn of events and draw in additional interest nearby. Local area contribution by private ventures makes a feeling of solidarity, shared values, and common help, cultivating serious areas of strength for a texture.

Private companies frequently partake in nearby occasions, support sports groups, and backing magnanimous associations. These exercises construct spans between private companies and their networks, further reinforcing the bond. At the point when private companies are effectively engaged with local area improvement, occupants are bound to help these undertakings through their support, making a harmonious relationship.

Moreover, private companies frequently add to local area improvement by offering special items and administrations that take care of neighborhood needs and inclinations. They comprehend the particular difficulties and open doors present in their networks, making them strategically set up to make arrangements that address neighborhood issues. Whether a local pastry kitchen gives new bread day to day or a home improvement shop that stocks things pertinent to the neighborhood environment, independent ventures increase the value of the local area by meeting these exceptional requirements.

The feeling of spot and personality encouraged by private companies is instrumental in local area attachment. At the point when occupants have a unique interaction with their nearby private ventures, they are bound to participate in local area exercises, support nearby drives, and team up with neighbors. Private companies act as get-together places, where inhabitants shop as well as interface with their neighbors, reinforcing the social texture of the local area.

In a quickly changing worldwide scene, the idea of strengthening with regards to local area contribution isn't static. It develops in light of arising difficulties and valuable open doors. For instance, the advanced change has essentially modified the independent venture strengthening scene. The approach of the web and online business has opened up new roads for independent companies to interface with their networks and arrive at a worldwide client base. Internet promoting and deals stages have permitted even the littlest endeavors to keep a web-based presence and cultivate a feeling of local area with their clients.

Maintainability is one more advancing element of private company strengthening with regards to local area advancement. With expanding accentuation on naturally capable practices and moral business direct, independent companies that embrace manageability add to a better planet as well as draw in a developing client base that esteems these standards. Enabling private companies to participate in maintainability drives helps the climate as well as cultivates a feeling of shared liability and local area contribution.

Government approaches and guidelines additionally adjust to address new difficulties and valuable open doors in the domain of local area contribution. For instance, during the Coronavirus pandemic, numerous states presented alleviation programs and monetary help to assist private companies with staying dynamic and drew in with their networks during testing times. These actions exhibited the adaptability of independent venture strengthening systems, as states immediately prepared to give fundamental guide during a period of scarcity.

The importance of enabling private ventures to draw in with their networks is clear with regards to restricted collaborations as well as on a more extensive scale. Private companies are fundamental parts of public economies, contributing altogether to Gross domestic product and occupation creation. By reinforcing private companies and empowering them to effectively partake in local area advancement, we support the underpinning of our public economies, guaranteeing their versatility and flexibility notwithstanding financial difficulties.

Moreover, private companies assume a fundamental part in worldwide financial frameworks. Their commitments to worldwide exchange and trade are significant, and their dynamic association in local area improvement upgrades their worldwide standing. Enabling private ventures to draw in with their networks cultivates local area attachment as well as enhances .

3.1 Small Businesses as Cornerstones of Communities

Independent companies, frequently portrayed by their unobtrusive size and confined presence, act as the foundations of networks. These undertakings go past their financial job; they are essential parts of the social texture, encouraging a feeling of personality, having a place, and shared values inside the neighborhoods they occupy. In this investigation, we dig into the complex connection between private companies and networks, accentuating the essential job these undertakings play in local area advancement, attachment, and social safeguarding.

Independent companies, ordinarily characterized as those with less than 500 workers, lay out and keep up with close associations with their networks, clients, and providers. This nearness and network empower private companies to have a profound comprehension of nearby necessities and inclinations, permitting them to fit their items and administrations to fulfill explicit needs. This limited way to deal with business tasks prompts local area driven arrangements as well as cultivates a significant feeling of association and common help.

Perhaps of the most obvious manner by which independent companies add to their networks is through work creation. These undertakings are significant wellsprings of business open doors, extending to different employment opportunity prospects, from passage level situations to administrative jobs. By recruiting people from the local area, private ventures diminish joblessness rates as well as fabricate more grounded social connections among managers and workers. This restricted way to deal with employing cultivates a feeling of having a place and mutual perspective, adding to local area improvement and union.

Moreover, independent ventures frequently focus on nearby employing, which upgrades local area improvement and adds to the financial prosperity of the district. They draw in with occupants, employing people who live in similar areas, grasp the particular necessities and inclinations of their customer base, and effectively take part in local area life. This limited way to deal with business cultivates a feeling of spot and character, fortifying the social texture of the local area.

Notwithstanding position creation, private ventures likewise participate in humanitarian exercises and local area contribution. Numerous entrepreneurs live in similar networks where they work their organizations, making them by and by put resources into the prosperity of the area. They frequently support nearby occasions, support beneficent associations, and take part in drives that address local area needs. These commitments go past financial exchanges and mirror a pledge to local area advancement and improvement.

Independent companies are not simply financial elements; they are essential pieces of the social texture. Their restricted presence, local area commitment, and customized administrations make an extraordinary feeling of spot and character. Clients frequently have individual associations with entrepreneurs and workers, encouraging a sensation of trust, having a place, and shared values. This feeling of association rises above simple exchanges and encourages a more profound connection between the local area and its independent ventures.

Engaging private ventures to add to local area improvement and union includes a few aspects. Admittance to monetary assets is fundamental, as it empowers private ventures to put resources into work creation and local area inclusion. Strengthening incorporates different types of funding, for example, conventional bank advances, investment, crowdfunding, or microloans, guaranteeing that independent ventures can tie down the vital cash-flow to help local area improvement drives.

Smoothing out guidelines is one more significant element of private venture strengthening with regards to local area association. Decreasing the managerial weight on independent ventures and making consistence with guidelines more clear and productive permits these endeavors to devote additional time and assets to local area drives. The objective is to establish a climate where private companies can draw in with their networks without over the top administrative requirements.

Tending to abberations in market power between private companies and bigger organizations is crucial for engaging private ventures to assume a functioning part in local area advancement. Approaches that advance fair contest, safeguard against monopolistic practices, and set out open doors for private companies to team up and frame coalitions can even the odds. A fair commercial center guarantees that independent ventures have the assets and impact to successfully draw in with their networks.

Building a strong environment of help is instrumental in private company strengthening for local area contribution. Entrepreneurs can benefit enormously from business warning administrations, mentorship programs, and systems administration open doors. Associating them with experienced guides and companions considers information sharing, best practice trade, and common help, at last prompting more compelling local area commitment.

Encouraging a steady and comprehensive business climate is likewise of fundamental significance with regards to local area improvement. Perceiving the one of a kind commitments of private companies and recognizing their job in nearby and worldwide economies can energize local area support, purchaser commitment, and a better business environment. At the point when private companies feel upheld by their networks and state run administrations, they are bound to participate in local area improvement drives.

The effect of enabling independent companies to draw in with their networks stretches out a long ways past the singular level. At the point when private ventures effectively add to local area improvement, they make a chain response of advantages. These commitments not just upgrade the general personal satisfaction for nearby occupants yet in addition animate monetary turn of events and draw in additional interest nearby. Local area contribution by private companies makes a feeling of solidarity, shared values, and common help, encouraging areas of strength for a texture.

Private ventures frequently partake in neighborhood occasions, support sports groups, and backing magnanimous associations. These exercises construct spans between private companies and their networks, further fortifying the bond. At the point when private companies are effectively engaged with local area improvement, occupants are bound to help these undertakings through their support, making a harmonious relationship.

Furthermore, private companies frequently add to local area improvement by offering special items and administrations that take care of neighborhood needs and inclinations. They comprehend the particular difficulties and open doors present in their networks, making them strategically situated to make arrangements that address neighborhood issues. Whether a local pastry shop gives new bread everyday or a home improvement shop that stocks things pertinent to the neighborhood environment, independent companies enhance the local area by meeting these exceptional necessities.

The feeling of spot and personality encouraged by private companies is instrumental in local area union. At the point when occupants have a special interaction with their nearby private companies, they are bound to take part in local area exercises, support nearby drives, and team up with neighbors. Independent ventures act as get-together places, where occupants shop as well as interface with their neighbors, fortifying the social texture of the local area.

In a quickly changing worldwide scene, the idea of strengthening with regards to local area contribution isn't static. It develops because of arising difficulties and valuable open doors. For instance, the computerized change has altogether adjusted the independent company strengthening scene. The appearance of the web and internet business has opened up new roads for private companies to interface with their networks and arrive at a worldwide client base. Internet promoting and deals stages have permitted even the littlest endeavors to keep a web-based presence and encourage a feeling of local area with their clients.

Maintainability is one more advancing element of private company strengthening with regards to local area advancement. With expanding accentuation on naturally mindful practices and moral business direct, private ventures that embrace manageability add to a better planet as well as draw in a developing client base that esteems these standards. Enabling private ventures to take part in maintainability drives helps the climate as well as encourages a feeling of shared liability and local area contribution.

Government approaches and guidelines additionally adjust to address new difficulties and valuable open doors in the domain of local area association. For instance, during the Coronavirus pandemic, numerous state run administrations presented alleviation programs and monetary help to assist independent ventures with staying dynamic and drew in with their networks during testing times. These actions displayed the adaptability of private company strengthening techniques, as states immediately prepared to give fundamental guide during a period of scarcity.

The importance of enabling private ventures to draw in with their networks is obvious with regards to restricted connections as well as on a more extensive scale. Independent ventures are fundamental parts of public economies, contributing altogether to Gross domestic product and occupation creation. By fortifying private ventures and empowering them to effectively take part in local area improvement, we support the underpinning of our public economies, guaranteeing their versatility and flexibility even with financial difficulties.

Besides, private ventures assume a crucial part in worldwide monetary frameworks. Their commitments to worldwide exchange and business are significant, and their dynamic contribution in local area advancement upgrades their worldwide standing. Enabling private ventures to draw in with their networks cultivates local area attachment as well as advances the interconnected worldwide community.

3.2 Building Cultural Identity and Trust

Private companies, frequently described by their humble size and confined presence, are instrumental in building social personality and trust inside their networks. These endeavors go past their monetary job; they are indispensable parts of the social texture, cultivating a feeling of personality, having a place, and shared values. Private ventures reflect and praise the variety and special social parts of the networks they serve. In this investigation, we dig into the diverse connection between private companies and social personality, underlining the crucial job these endeavors play in safeguarding and celebrating neighborhood culture and supporting trust among occupants.

Independent ventures, commonly characterized as those with less than 500 workers, lay out and keep up with close associations with their networks, clients, and providers. This nearness and network empower independent ventures to have a profound comprehension of nearby necessities and inclinations, permitting them to fit their items and administrations to fulfill explicit needs. This limited way to deal with business tasks prompts local area driven arrangements as well as encourages a significant feeling of association and common help.

Quite possibly of the most obvious manner by which independent companies add to their networks is through work creation. These endeavors are urgent wellsprings of business open doors, extending to assorted employment opportunity prospects, from section level situations to administrative jobs. By recruiting people from the local area, private ventures diminish joblessness rates as well as fabricate more grounded social connections among managers and representatives. This confined way to deal with employing cultivates a feeling of having a place and common perspective, adding to local area improvement and union.

Besides, private companies frequently focus on nearby recruiting, which improves local area advancement and adds to the financial prosperity of the district. They draw in with occupants, recruiting people who live in similar areas, grasp the particular requirements and inclinations of their customer base, and effectively partake in local area life. This restricted way to deal with business cultivates a feeling of spot and character, fortifying the social texture of the local area.

Notwithstanding position creation, private companies additionally participate in altruistic exercises and local area association. Numerous entrepreneurs live in similar networks where they work their organizations, making them actually put resources into the prosperity of the area. They frequently support nearby occasions, support magnanimous associations, and take part in drives that address local area needs. These commitments go past financial exchanges and mirror a promise to local area advancement and improvement.

Independent companies are not simply monetary substances; they are indispensable pieces of the social texture. Their restricted presence, local area commitment, and customized administrations make an exceptional feeling of spot and character. Clients frequently have individual associations with entrepreneurs and workers, cultivating a sensation of trust, having a place, and shared values. This feeling of association rises above simple exchanges and cultivates a more profound connection between the local area and its independent ventures.

Engaging independent ventures to add to social personality and trust includes a few aspects. Admittance to monetary assets is fundamental, as it empowers private companies to put resources into social conservation and local area inclusion. Strengthening incorporates different types of funding, for example, customary bank advances, investment, crowdfunding, or microloans, guaranteeing that independent ventures can tie down the important money to help social drives.

Smoothing out guidelines is one more pivotal component of private company strengthening with regards to social character. Diminishing the regulatory weight on private ventures and making consistence with guidelines more direct and proficient permits these endeavors to devote additional time and assets to social safeguarding and local area inclusion. The objective is to establish a climate where private companies can draw in with their networks without unnecessary administrative requirements.

Tending to abberations in market power between private companies and bigger partnerships is significant for engaging independent companies to assume a functioning part in safeguarding neighborhood culture. Approaches that advance fair contest, safeguard against monopolistic practices, and set out open doors for independent ventures to celebrate and protect neighborhood customs can even the odds. A fair commercial center guarantees that independent ventures have the assets and impact to successfully draw in with their networks.

Building a strong biological system of help is instrumental in private venture strengthening for social character. Entrepreneurs can benefit enormously from business warning administrations, mentorship programs, and systems administration open doors that empower them to celebrate and save nearby culture. Associating them with experienced coaches and friends considers information sharing, best practice trade, and common help, eventually prompting more viable social drives.

Cultivating a strong and comprehensive business climate is likewise of principal significance with regards to social character. Perceiving the remarkable commitments of private companies and recognizing their job in nearby and worldwide economies can empower local area support, customer commitment, and a better business environment that permits private ventures to celebrate and safeguard neighborhood culture. At the point when private companies feel upheld by their networks and state run administrations, they are bound to take part in social safeguarding drives.

The effect of engaging private ventures to celebrate and safeguard neighborhood culture stretches out a long ways past the singular level. At the point when private ventures effectively add to social personality, they make a chain response of advantages. These commitments not just improve the general personal satisfaction for nearby occupants yet in addition animate monetary turn of events and draw in additional interest nearby. Celebrating nearby culture by independent companies cultivates a feeling of solidarity, shared values, and common trust, reinforcing the social texture.

Private ventures frequently take part in nearby occasions, support social celebrations, and backing drives that celebrate neighborhood customs. These exercises construct spans between private ventures and their networks, further reinforcing the bond. At the point when independent ventures effectively add to social character, inhabitants are bound to help these endeavors through their support, making a cooperative relationship.

Moreover, independent companies frequently add to social character by offering remarkable items and administrations that reflect nearby customs and legacy. They comprehend the particular social components and inclinations of their networks, making them strategically set up to make arrangements that celebrate and protect nearby culture. Whether an eatery serves conventional provincial dishes or a store that sells handmade products, independent ventures increase the value of the local area by saving and celebrating nearby culture.

The feeling of spot and personality cultivated by private ventures is instrumental in social protection. At the point when occupants have a unique interaction with their nearby private ventures that celebrate and protect neighborhood culture, they are bound to participate in social exercises, support nearby drives, and invest heavily in their social legacy. Private ventures act as social center points, where occupants shop as well as drench themselves in the nearby practices and praise their common social character.

In a quickly changing worldwide scene, the idea of strengthening with regards to social personality isn't static. It advances because of arising difficulties and open doors. For instance, the advanced change has altogether modified the private venture strengthening scene. The approach of the web and internet business has opened up new roads for independent ventures to celebrate and protect nearby culture and arrive at a worldwide client base. Web based showcasing and deals stages have permitted even the littlest undertakings to keep an internet based presence and encourage a feeling of social personality with their clients.

Maintainability is one more developing element of private company strengthening with regards to social character. With expanding accentuation on naturally capable practices and moral business direct, independent ventures that celebrate and protect neighborhood culture add to a better planet as well as draw in a developing client base that esteems these standards. Enabling private ventures to participate in manageability drives that celebrate nearby culture upgrades their standing and cultivates a feeling of shared liability and social conservation.

Government strategies and guidelines likewise adjust to address new difficulties and potential open doors in the domain of social conservation. For instance, during the Coronavirus pandemic, numerous legislatures presented alleviation programs and monetary help to help private companies that celebrate and safeguard neighborhood culture stay dynamic and drew in with their networks during testing times. These actions displayed the adaptability of independent venture strengthening techniques, as legislatures immediately prepared to give fundamental guide during a period of scarcity.

The importance of engaging private companies to celebrate and save neighborhood culture is obvious with regards to restricted communications as well as on a more extensive scale. Independent ventures are fundamental parts of public economies, contributing altogether to Gross domestic product and occupation creation. By fortifying private ventures and empowering them to effectively take part in social conservation, we support the underpinning of our public economies, guaranteeing their resilience.

3.3 The Social Fabric of Local Economies

Private companies, frequently portrayed by their unassuming size and confined presence, are indispensable to the social texture of nearby economies. They go past their financial job; they are fundamental parts of the networks they serve, forming the way of life, encouraging a feeling of character, and supporting social associations. In this investigation, we dig into the complex connection between private ventures and the social texture of nearby economies, accentuating the crucial job these endeavors play in local area improvement, union, and strength.

Private ventures, normally characterized as those with less than 500 representatives, lay out and keep up with close associations with their networks, clients, and providers. This nearness and network empower private ventures to have a profound comprehension of nearby necessities and inclinations, permitting them to fit their items and administrations to fulfill explicit needs. This confined way to deal with business tasks prompts local area driven arrangements as well as encourages a significant feeling of association and common help.

Perhaps of the most clear manner by which private ventures add to their networks is through work creation. These ventures are critical wellsprings of business potential open doors, extending to different employment opportunity prospects, from passage level situations to administrative jobs. By recruiting people from the local area, independent companies diminish joblessness rates as well as fabricate more grounded social connections among managers and representatives. This restricted way to deal with employing cultivates a feeling of having a place and mutual perspective, adding to local area improvement and union.

Besides, independent companies frequently focus on neighborhood recruiting, which upgrades local area improvement and adds to the financial prosperity of the district. They draw in with occupants, recruiting people who live in similar areas, grasp the particular requirements and inclinations of their customers, and effectively take part in local area life.

This restricted way to deal with work cultivates a feeling of spot and personality, fortifying the social texture of the local area.

Notwithstanding position creation, private ventures likewise participate in charitable exercises and local area association. Numerous entrepreneurs live in similar networks where they work their organizations, making them by and by put resources into the prosperity of the area. They frequently support neighborhood occasions, support altruistic associations, and take part in drives that address local area needs. These commitments go past financial exchanges and mirror a pledge to local area advancement and improvement.

Private companies are not simply financial elements; they are essential pieces of the social texture. Their restricted presence, local area commitment, and customized administrations make a novel feeling of spot and personality. Clients frequently have individual associations with entrepreneurs and representatives, encouraging a sensation of trust, having a place, and shared values. This feeling of association rises above simple exchanges and encourages a more profound connection between the local area and its private companies.

Enabling private companies to add to local area advancement and attachment includes a few aspects. Admittance to monetary assets is fundamental, as it empowers private ventures to put resources into work creation and local area inclusion. Strengthening incorporates different types of funding, for example, conventional bank credits, investment, crowdfunding, or microloans, guaranteeing that private companies can tie down the important cash-flow to help local area improvement drives.

Smoothing out guidelines is one more urgent component of private company strengthening with regards to local area contribution. Decreasing the regulatory weight on independent companies and making consistence with guidelines more clear and proficient permits these undertakings to commit additional time and assets to local area drives. The objective is to establish a climate where private ventures can draw in with their networks without unnecessary regulatory requirements.

Tending to variations in market power between private companies and bigger enterprises is crucial for engaging independent ventures to assume a functioning part in local area improvement. Arrangements that advance fair contest, safeguard against monopolistic practices, and set out open doors for private ventures to team up and shape collusions can even the odds. A fair commercial center guarantees that independent companies have the assets and impact to really draw in with their networks.

Building a powerful environment of help is instrumental in private company strengthening for local area contribution. Entrepreneurs can benefit significantly from business warning administrations, mentorship programs, and systems administration open doors. Interfacing them with experienced tutors and friends considers information sharing, best practice trade, and common help, eventually prompting more viable local area commitment.

Cultivating a steady and comprehensive business climate is likewise of vital significance with regards to local area improvement. Perceiving the extraordinary commitments of private ventures and recognizing their job in neighborhood and worldwide economies can energize local area support, customer commitment, and a better business environment. At the point when private ventures feel upheld by their networks and state run administrations, they are bound to take part in local area advancement drives.

The effect of enabling independent ventures to draw in with their networks reaches out a long ways past the singular level. At the point when private ventures effectively add to local area improvement, they make a chain response of advantages. These commitments not just upgrade the general personal satisfaction for nearby occupants yet in addition animate monetary turn of events and draw in additional interest nearby. Local area contribution by private companies makes a feeling of solidarity, shared values, and common trust, reinforcing the social texture.

Private companies frequently take part in nearby occasions, support sports groups, and backing magnanimous associations. These exercises fabricate spans between independent companies and their networks, further fortifying the bond. At the point when private ventures are effectively engaged with local area improvement, inhabitants are bound to help these endeavors through their support, making a harmonious relationship.

Moreover, private ventures frequently add to local area improvement by offering remarkable items and administrations that take special care of nearby requirements and inclinations. They comprehend the particular difficulties and valuable open doors present in their networks, making them strategically set up to make arrangements that address nearby issues. Whether a local pastry kitchen gives new bread everyday or a home improvement shop that stocks things pertinent to the neighborhood environment, independent ventures increase the value of the local area by meeting these exceptional requirements.

The feeling of spot and character encouraged by private companies is instrumental in local area union. At the point when occupants have a unique interaction with their nearby private companies, they are bound to take part in local area exercises, support nearby drives, and team up with neighbors. Private companies act as get-together places, where occupants shop as well as interface with their neighbors, reinforcing the social texture of the local area.

In a quickly changing worldwide scene, the idea of strengthening with regards to local area contribution isn't static. It advances in light of arising difficulties and potential open doors. For instance, the advanced change has fundamentally adjusted the private company strengthening scene. The approach of the web and internet business has opened up new roads for independent ventures to interface with their networks and arrive at a worldwide client base. Internet showcasing and deals stages have permitted even the littlest endeavors to keep a web-based presence and cultivate a feeling of local area with their clients.

Maintainability is one more advancing component of private venture strengthening with regards to local area improvement. With expanding accentuation on naturally capable practices and moral business lead, independent ventures that embrace supportability add to a better planet as well as draw in a developing client base that esteems these standards. Enabling private companies to take part in supportability drives helps the climate as well as cultivates a feeling of shared liability and local area contribution.

Government arrangements and guidelines additionally adjust to address new difficulties and potential open doors in the domain of local area contribution. For instance, during the Coronavirus pandemic, numerous states presented alleviation programs and monetary help to assist private companies with staying dynamic and drew in with their networks during testing times. These actions displayed the adaptability of private company strengthening procedures, as states immediately prepared to give fundamental guide during a period of scarcity.

The pertinence of enabling private companies to draw in with their networks is clear with regards to confined collaborations as well as on a more extensive scale. Private ventures are fundamental parts of public economies, contributing altogether to Gross domestic product and occupation creation. By fortifying private companies and empowering them to effectively take part in local area advancement, we reinforce the groundwork of our public economies, guaranteeing their strength and versatility despite monetary difficulties.

Moreover, private ventures assume an essential part in worldwide monetary frameworks. Their commitments to worldwide exchange and business are significant, and their dynamic contribution in local area improvement upgrades their worldwide standing. Enabling private ventures to draw in with their networks encourages local area attachment as well as improves the interconnected worldwide .

Chapter 4

Sustainability and Small Businesses

Private companies, frequently portrayed by their unassuming size and confined presence, assume a vital part in the supportability scene. These ventures go past their monetary job; they are fundamental parts of the networks they serve, and their activities essentially influence the climate and the prosperity of society. In this investigation, we dig into the multi-layered connection between private companies and supportability, underlining the imperative job these undertakings play in natural obligation, social effect, and monetary flexibility.

Private companies, normally characterized as those with less than 500 workers, lay out and keep up with close associations with their networks, clients, and providers. This nearness and network empower private companies to have a profound comprehension of nearby requirements and inclinations, permitting them to fit their items and administrations to fulfill explicit needs. This confined way to deal with business tasks prompts local area driven arrangements as well as encourages a significant feeling of association and shared help.

Perhaps of the most clear manner by which independent ventures add to maintainability is through their confined way to deal with creation and utilization. Private companies frequently source their materials and items locally, lessening the carbon impression related with transportation and supporting nearby providers. Furthermore, they will quite often focus on mindful obtaining, picking providers with supportable practices, which, thus, empowers economical practices all through the inventory network.

Besides, independent ventures as often as possible hug harmless to the ecosystem rehearses, like energy productivity, squander decrease, and reusing. Their more limited size and adaptability frequently empower them to embrace supportable measures more quickly and effectively than bigger companies. Whether it's a little bread shop utilizing privately processed flour or a local supermarket obtaining occasional, privately developed produce, independent companies add to maintainability by decreasing the ecological effect of their tasks.

Private ventures likewise assume a basic part in the advancement of capable utilization. They will generally zero in on the quality and life span of their items, as well as offering customized types of assistance, which can prompt a more manageable buyer outlook. By offering items that are dependable, private companies urge clients to put resources into more excellent things that are less inclined to wind up in landfills. This way to deal with business cultivates maintainability through mindful creation as well as through scrupulous utilization.

Notwithstanding their natural commitments, private companies are many times profoundly implanted in the social texture of their networks. Numerous entrepreneurs live in similar neighborhoods where they work their organizations, making them actually put resources into the prosperity of the area. They as often as possible take part in generous exercises, support neighborhood occasions, support beneficent associations, and take part in drives that address local area needs. These commitments go past monetary exchanges and mirror a promise to local area improvement and social maintainability.

Independent companies are not simply monetary elements; they are necessary pieces of the social texture. Their restricted presence, local area commitment, and customized administrations make an extraordinary feeling of spot and character. Clients frequently have individual associations with entrepreneurs and representatives, cultivating a sensation of trust, having a place, and shared values. This feeling of association rises above simple exchanges and encourages a more profound connection between the local area and its private ventures.

Engaging independent ventures to add to manageability includes a few aspects. Admittance to monetary assets is fundamental, as it empowers private ventures to put resources into economical practices. Strengthening incorporates different types of funding, for example, conventional bank credits, investment, crowdfunding, or microloans, guaranteeing that independent companies can tie down the essential cashflow to help manageability drives.

Smoothing out guidelines is one more urgent component of private company strengthening with regards to supportability. Decreasing the authoritative weight on private ventures and making consistence with natural guidelines more clear and effective permits these endeavors to devote additional time and assets to manageability endeavors. The objective is to establish a climate where private ventures can participate in economical practices without unreasonable regulatory limitations.

Tending to differences in market power between private companies and bigger enterprises is significant for engaging private companies to assume a functioning part in maintainability. Strategies that advance fair rivalry, safeguard against monopolistic practices, and set out open doors for independent companies to embrace and advance manageable practices can even the odds. A fair commercial center guarantees that private ventures have the assets and impact to really draw in with manageability.

Building a vigorous biological system of help is instrumental in private venture strengthening for manageability. Entrepreneurs can benefit incredibly from business warning administrations, mentorship programs, and systems administration valuable open doors that empower them to take on supportable practices. Associating them with experienced coaches and companions takes into account information sharing, best practice trade, and common help, at last prompting more successful manageability drives.

Encouraging a strong and comprehensive business climate is likewise of foremost significance with regards to maintainability. Perceiving the one of a kind commitments of private companies and recognizing their part in neighborhood and worldwide economies can energize local area support, buyer commitment, and a better business environment that permits independent ventures to embrace and advance maintainable practices. At the point when private companies feel upheld by their networks and states, they are bound to take part in supportability drives.

The effect of engaging private ventures to add to maintainability reaches out a long ways past the singular level. At the point when private companies effectively take on and advance maintainable practices, they make a chain response of advantages. These commitments not just upgrade the general personal satisfaction for nearby occupants yet additionally animate financial turn of events and draw in additional interest nearby. Manageability endeavors by private companies make a feeling of solidarity, shared values, and common trust, reinforcing the social texture.

Private companies frequently partake in neighborhood occasions, support natural drives, and backing magnanimous associations that emphasis on maintainability. These exercises fabricate spans between independent companies and their networks, further fortifying the bond. At the point when private companies are effectively engaged with maintainability, occupants are bound to help these endeavors through their support, making a cooperative relationship.

Also, independent ventures frequently add to maintainability by offering eco-accommodating items and administrations. They figure out the rising significance of natural obligation and take special care of the inclinations of clients who esteem manageability. Whether it's a shop selling morally obtained clothing or a neighborhood eatery serving natural and privately developed food, independent companies enhance the local area by giving maintainable choices.

The feeling of spot and personality encouraged by private ventures is instrumental in the reception and advancement of supportable practices. At the point when inhabitants have a special interaction with their neighborhood private companies, they are bound to embrace maintainability drives and settle on ecologically capable decisions. Private companies act as centers for supportability training, where inhabitants shop as well as find out about eco-accommodating items and works on, reinforcing the social texture of the local area.

In a quickly changing worldwide scene, the idea of strengthening with regards to manageability isn't static. It develops in light of arising difficulties and open doors. For instance, the computerized change has essentially modified the private company strengthening scene. The coming of the web and online business has opened up new roads for independent ventures to take on and advance feasible practices and arrive at a worldwide client base. Internet showcasing and deals stages have permitted even the littlest endeavors to keep a web-based presence and cultivate manageability mindfulness with their clients.

Supportability is one more developing component of private venture strengthening. With expanding accentuation on earth capable practices and moral business lead, private companies that embrace manageability add to a better planet as well as draw in a developing client base that esteems these standards. Enabling private companies to take part in supportability drives helps the climate as well as encourages a feeling of shared liability and local area contribution.

Government arrangements and guidelines additionally adjust to address new difficulties and amazing open doors in the domain of manageability. For instance, during the Coronavirus pandemic, numerous states presented alleviation programs and monetary help to assist private companies with staying dynamic and drew in with their networks during testing times. These actions exhibited the adaptability of independent venture strengthening methodologies, as states immediately prepared to give fundamental guide during a period of scarcity.

4.1 Small Businesses as Sustainable Pioneers

Private ventures, frequently described by their humble size and restricted presence, are arising as practical trailblazers in a world progressively centered around ecological obligation and social effect. These endeavors go past their monetary job; they are indispensable parts of the networks they serve, and their activities fundamentally influence the climate and the prosperity of society. In this investigation, we dive into the multi-layered connection between private companies and supportability, stressing the fundamental job these ventures play in advocating eco-accommodating works on, encouraging social effect, and advancing financial versatility.

Private ventures, commonly characterized as those with less than 500 workers, lay out and keep up with close associations with their networks, clients, and providers. This vicinity and network empower private companies to have a profound comprehension of neighborhood needs and inclinations, permitting them to fit their items and administrations to fulfill explicit needs. This confined way to deal with business tasks prompts local area driven arrangements as well as encourages a significant feeling of association and shared help.

Perhaps of the most clear manner by which private companies add to maintainability is through their confined way to deal with creation and utilization. Private ventures frequently source their materials and items locally, diminishing the carbon impression related with transportation and supporting neighborhood providers. Moreover, they will quite often focus on capable obtaining, picking providers with manageable practices, which, thusly, supports reasonable practices all through the inventory network.

Private ventures likewise assume a crucial part in the advancement of mindful utilization. They will generally zero in on the quality and life span of their items, as well as offering customized types of assistance, which can prompt a more economical buyer outlook. By offering items that are solid, private companies urge clients to put resources into greater things that are less inclined to wind up in landfills. This way to deal with business encourages supportability through dependable creation as well as through faithful utilization.

Moreover, independent companies oftentimes embrace harmless to the ecosystem rehearses, like energy productivity, squander decrease, and reusing. Their more limited size and adaptability frequently empower them to take on feasible measures more quickly and effectively than bigger organizations. Whether it's a little pastry shop utilizing privately processed flour or a local supermarket obtaining occasional, privately developed produce, independent ventures add to maintainability by lessening the natural effect of their tasks.

Notwithstanding their ecological commitments, private ventures are much of the time profoundly implanted in the social texture of their networks. Numerous entrepreneurs live in similar neighborhoods where they work their organizations, making them actually put resources into the prosperity of the area. They oftentimes participate in humanitarian exercises, support neighborhood occasions, support beneficent associations, and take part in drives that address local area needs. These commitments go past financial exchanges and mirror a guarantee to local area improvement and social maintainability.

Independent companies are not simply financial substances; they are necessary pieces of the social texture. Their confined presence, local area commitment, and customized administrations make a one of a kind feeling of spot and character. Clients frequently have individual associations with entrepreneurs and representatives, encouraging a sensation of trust, having a place, and shared values. This feeling of association rises above simple exchanges and cultivates a more profound connection between the local area and its independent ventures.

Enabling independent ventures to add to maintainability includes a few aspects. Admittance to monetary assets is fundamental, as it empowers private companies to put resources into eco-accommodating practices. Strengthening incorporates different types of funding, for example, customary bank advances, investment, crowdfunding, or microloans, guaranteeing that private companies can tie down the important cash-flow to help maintainability drives.

Smoothing out guidelines is one more urgent element of private company strengthening with regards to manageability. Decreasing the regulatory weight on private companies and making consistence with ecological guidelines more clear and productive permits these ventures to commit additional time and assets to maintainability endeavors. The objective is to establish a climate where private ventures can participate in feasible practices without over the top administrative requirements.

Tending to abberations in market power between private ventures and bigger partnerships is crucial for enabling private ventures to assume a functioning part in manageability. Approaches that advance fair rivalry, safeguard against monopolistic practices, and set out open doors for private ventures to take on and advance feasible practices can even the odds. A reasonable commercial center guarantees that independent companies have the assets and impact to successfully draw in with manageability.

Building a strong environment of help is instrumental in private company strengthening for maintainability. Entrepreneurs can benefit significantly from business warning administrations, mentorship programs, and systems administration open doors that empower them to take on and advance reasonable practices. Interfacing them with experienced tutors and companions takes into account information sharing, best practice trade, and common help, eventually prompting more successful maintainability drives.

Cultivating a strong and comprehensive business climate is likewise of foremost significance with regards to manageability. Perceiving the special commitments of private companies and recognizing their part in neighborhood and worldwide economies can energize local area support, purchaser commitment, and a better business environment that permits independent ventures to embrace and advance feasible practices. At the point when private ventures feel upheld by their networks and states, they are bound to participate in maintainability drives.

The effect of enabling independent ventures to add to supportability reaches out a long ways past the singular level. At the point when private companies effectively take on and advance manageable practices, they make a chain response of advantages. These commitments not just upgrade the general personal satisfaction for neighborhood occupants yet additionally animate financial turn of events and draw in additional interest nearby. Maintainability endeavors by independent companies make a feeling of solidarity, shared values, and common trust, fortifying the social texture.

Private companies frequently take part in nearby occasions, support ecological drives, and backing beneficent associations that attention on maintainability. These exercises assemble spans between private companies and their networks, further fortifying the bond. At the point when private ventures are effectively engaged with manageability, occupants are bound to help these undertakings through their support, making a harmonious relationship.

Furthermore, private companies frequently add to supportability by offering eco-accommodating items and administrations. They grasp the rising significance of natural obligation and take special care of the inclinations of clients who esteem maintainability. Whether it's a shop selling morally obtained clothing or a neighborhood eatery serving natural and privately developed food, independent ventures increase the value of the local area by giving economical choices.

The feeling of spot and personality encouraged by private ventures is instrumental in the reception and advancement of reasonable practices. At the point when inhabitants have a special interaction with their neighborhood private ventures, they are bound to embrace maintainability drives and settle on naturally mindful decisions. Independent ventures act as center points for manageability instruction, where inhabitants shop as well as find out about eco-accommodating items and works on, reinforcing the social texture of the local area.

In a quickly changing worldwide scene, the idea of strengthening with regards to maintainability isn't static. It advances because of arising difficulties and open doors. For instance, the advanced change has altogether adjusted the independent venture strengthening scene. The approach of the web and internet business has opened up new roads for private ventures to embrace and advance feasible practices and arrive at a worldwide client base. Web based advertising and deals stages have permitted even the littlest ventures to keep an internet based presence and cultivate supportability mindfulness with their clients.

Manageability is one more developing component of independent venture strengthening. With expanding accentuation on earth capable practices and moral business lead, private ventures that embrace maintainability add to a better planet as well as draw in a developing client base that esteems these standards. Enabling private companies to take part in manageability drives helps the climate as well as encourages a feeling of shared liability and local area contribution.

Government approaches and guidelines additionally adjust to address new difficulties and potential open doors in the domain of manageability. For instance, during the Coronavirus pandemic, numerous state run administrations presented alleviation programs and monetary help to assist independent companies with staying dynamic and drew in with their networks during testing times. These actions exhibited the adaptability of private company strengthening methodologies, as states immediately prepared to give fundamental guide during a period of scarcity.

4.2 Local Sourcing and Reduced Carbon Footprint

The idea of supportability has become progressively huge lately, with a developing accentuation on diminishing fossil fuel byproducts and limiting the natural effect of human exercises. Private companies, frequently portrayed by their limited presence, play a novel part to play chasing maintainability. One of the critical manners by which independent companies add to maintainability is through their obligation to neighborhood obtaining, which can possibly fundamentally lessen carbon impressions and advance mindful utilization.

Private ventures, ordinarily characterized as those with less than 500 representatives, lay out and keep up with close associations with their networks, clients, and providers. This closeness and network empower them to have a profound comprehension of neighborhood needs and inclinations, permitting them to fit their items and administrations to fulfill explicit needs. Neighborhood obtaining is a characteristic expansion of this restricted way to deal with business tasks.

Neighborhood obtaining alludes to the act of acquiring merchandise, materials, and administrations from adjacent providers and makers. Independent companies frequently focus on neighborhood obtaining in light of multiple factors, including supporting the nearby economy, cultivating local area associations, and diminishing their natural effect. At the point when independent ventures pick neighborhood providers, they can essentially diminish the fossil fuel byproducts related with transportation and planned operations, making a positive commitment to manageability.

The decrease in transportation-related outflows is one of the essential ecological advantages of nearby obtaining. Customary stockpile chains for bigger enterprises frequently include the transportation of products over significant distances, once in a while even across global lines. This transportation requires significant energy utilization and is related with ozone depleting substance discharges that add to environmental change. Private ventures, by picking nearby providers, can diminish the distance over which products should be shipped, hence bringing down the carbon impression of their activities.

Also, neighborhood obtaining permits private companies to fabricate more grounded associations with nearby providers and makers. These connections are many times based on trust, shared values, and common help. The feeling of organization between private companies and neighborhood providers encourages capable obtaining rehearses, as the two players are put resources into the prosperity of the local area. This obligation to capable obtaining reaches out all through the production network, empowering moral and manageable practices.

Private companies that focus on nearby obtaining likewise add to the financial flexibility of their networks. By supporting close by ranchers, craftsmans, and producers, private ventures assist with guaranteeing the dependability and success of nearby economies. This monetary maintainability reinforces the social texture of the local area, as flourishing nearby organizations and providers make occupations and advance social prosperity.

Nearby obtaining lines up with the standards of mindful utilization and supports the development of a roundabout economy. Private companies frequently center around the quality and life span of their items, empowering clients to put resources into more excellent things that are less inclined to wind up in landfills. This approach cultivates supportability through capable creation as well as through faithful utilization, lessening waste and empowering a mentality of solidness and reuse.

For instance, a neighborhood bread kitchen that sources its flour from a close by plant and its organic products from nearby ranchers can fundamentally lessen its carbon impression contrasted with a bigger pastry shop that depends on fixings obtained from far off locales. Notwithstanding the ecological advantages, the neighborhood bread kitchen adds to the financial steadiness of the local area, upholds nearby agribusiness, and furnishes its clients with new, great items, advancing dependable utilization.

The accentuation on neighborhood obtaining is in arrangement with bigger supportability patterns. Across the globe, purchasers are progressively looking for items that are privately obtained, manageable, and naturally dependable. Private companies that embrace neighborhood obtaining rehearses are strategically set up to meet these customer inclinations and make an upper hand.

Engaging independent ventures to proceed with their obligation to neighborhood obtaining includes different aspects. Admittance to a different organization of neighborhood providers is crucial, as it permits private companies to find maintainable choices that line up with their qualities. Strengthening incorporates cultivating associations between independent ventures and nearby makers, giving a stage to joint effort and information sharing that advances capable obtaining.

Smoothing out guidelines to work with neighborhood obtaining is one more vital component of independent venture strengthening. Diminishing managerial impediments and making consistence with natural and obtaining guidelines more direct empowers private ventures to take part in supportable practices. The objective is to establish a climate where neighborhood obtaining is energized and upheld by government approaches.

Tending to variations in market power between private companies and bigger organizations is vital for engaging independent ventures to embrace nearby obtaining. Approaches that advance fair contest and set out open doors for private ventures to team up with neighborhood providers can even the odds. A reasonable commercial center guarantees that private companies have the assets and impact to really focus on neighborhood obtaining.

Building a vigorous biological system of help is instrumental in private company strengthening for nearby obtaining. Entrepreneurs can benefit enormously from admittance to assets and stages that associate them with neighborhood providers and makers. These organizations give amazing open doors to private ventures to find reasonable obtaining choices and take part in capable strategic approaches.

Cultivating a steady and comprehensive business climate is likewise of principal significance with regards to neighborhood obtaining. Perceiving the novel commitments of private ventures and recognizing their part in neighborhood and worldwide economies can empower local area support, purchaser commitment, and a better business environment that permits independent ventures to focus on nearby obtaining.

The effect of enabling independent companies to embrace neighborhood obtaining stretches out past ecological supportability. At the point when private ventures effectively support nearby providers and makers, they fortify the social texture of the local area. These associations construct trust, shared values, and common help, adding to local area improvement and monetary flexibility.

Private ventures frequently partake in neighborhood occasions, support local area drives, and backing altruistic associations that attention on capable obtaining and maintainability. These exercises assemble spans between private ventures, nearby providers, and their networks, further reinforcing the bond. At the point when private ventures effectively participate in nearby obtaining, occupants are bound to help these undertakings through their support, making a harmonious relationship that encourages maintainability.

The feeling of spot and character cultivated by private ventures is instrumental in the reception and advancement of nearby obtaining. At the point when occupants have a unique interaction with their neighborhood independent ventures and providers, they are bound to embrace maintainable obtaining practices and pursue mindful utilization decisions. Private companies act as centers for maintainable obtaining instruction, where inhabitants shop as well as find out about the significance of neighborhood obtaining, reinforcing the social texture of the local area.

In a quickly changing worldwide scene, the idea of strengthening with regards to nearby obtaining isn't static. It advances in light of arising difficulties and potential open doors. For instance, the advanced change has altogether modified the independent venture strengthening scene. The approach of the web and internet business has opened up new roads for independent ventures to interface with nearby providers, advance neighborhood obtaining, and arrive at a worldwide client base. Internet advertising and deals stages have permitted even the littlest undertakings to keep a web-based presence and encourage nearby obtaining mindfulness with their clients.

Nearby obtaining is one more advancing element of independent company strengthening. With expanding accentuation on ecologically dependable practices and moral obtaining, private companies that embrace neighborhood obtaining add to a better planet as well as draw in a developing client base that esteems these standards. Enabling private companies to take part in neighborhood obtaining drives helps the climate as well as encourages a feeling of shared liability and local area contribution.

Government strategies and guidelines additionally adjust to address new difficulties and valuable open doors in the domain of neighborhood obtaining. For instance, during the Coronavirus pandemic, numerous states presented alleviation programs and monetary help to assist private ventures with staying dynamic and drew in with their nearby providers and networks during testing times. These actions exhibited the adaptability of independent company strengthening techniques, as states immediately prepared to give fundamental guide during a period of scarcity.

The significance of enabling private ventures to embrace neighborhood obtaining is clear with regards to restricted collaborations as well as on a more extensive scale. Private ventures are fundamental parts of public economies, contributing essentially to Gross domestic product and occupation creation. By reinforcing private companies and empowering them to effectively focus on neighborhood obtaining, we support the underpinning of our public economies, guaranteeing their strength and flexibility even with monetary difficulties.

4.3 Ethical Practices and Environmental Responsibility

In a period set apart by developing natural worries and an elevated feeling of social obligation, moral practices and ecological obligation have become foremost. Private companies, frequently well established in their networks, are strategically set up to assume a huge part in tending to these difficulties. Their confined presence permits them to encourage moral practices and ecological obligation in a manner that significantly affects the prosperity of both nearby networks and the planet.

Independent companies, normally characterized as those with less than 500 workers, lay out and keep up with close associations with their networks, clients, and providers. This nearness and network empower them to have a profound comprehension of nearby requirements and inclinations, encouraging a climate helpful for moral practices and ecological obligation. Private companies frequently act as impetuses for positive change, advancing maintainability and moral lead in their areas of activity.

The reception of moral practices by independent ventures goes past simple consistence with lawful prerequisites. It frequently includes a pledge to reasonableness, trustworthiness, and straightforwardness in their tasks. Moral organizations focus on the prosperity of their workers, clients, and the more extensive local area, intending to make a positive effect as opposed to zeroing in exclusively on benefit expansion.

Moral practices envelop different parts of business direct, including fair work rehearses, moral obtaining, and capable promoting. Independent ventures frequently try to make a work environment culture that values variety, correspondence, and representative prosperity. They intend to approach their representatives with deference, guaranteeing fair wages, safe working circumstances, and open doors for proficient development.

Besides, moral obtaining is a basic part of private ventures' obligation to moral practices. Entrepreneurs regularly draw in with nearby providers and makers who share their qualities. This coordinated effort frequently brings about maintainable and morally obtained materials and items. Moral obtaining stretches out all through the inventory network, guaranteeing that private ventures support dependable practices inside their tasks as well as among their providers.

Independent ventures are likewise aware of mindful advertising and client commitment. They focus on honest publicizing, staying away from misleading practices that could hurt purchasers.

Moral advertising conveys the worth of the items or administrations sincerely and straightforwardly, making entrust with clients. Independent companies endeavor to fabricate connections in view of common regard and shared values, cultivating a reliable client base.

Private ventures habitually champion ecological obligation, perceiving their job in decreasing the natural effect of their tasks. They embrace eco-accommodating practices, like energy proficiency, squander decrease, and reusing, as well as capable obtaining and maintainable item contributions. Their more limited size and adaptability empower them to adjust to harmless to the ecosystem rehearses more quickly and effectively than bigger organizations.

One of the huge commitments of independent ventures to ecological obligation is their emphasis on nearby obtaining. By acquiring products, materials, and administrations from neighboring providers, private companies decrease the carbon impression related with transportation and operations. The decrease in transportation-related discharges is one of the essential ecological advantages of nearby obtaining. Independent companies that focus on neighborhood obtaining can essentially bring down the carbon impression of their tasks, making a significant commitment to maintainability.

For instance, a neighborhood bread kitchen that sources its flour from a close by plant and its natural products from nearby ranchers can essentially lessen its carbon impression contrasted with a bigger pastry shop that depends on fixings obtained from far off districts. Notwithstanding the natural advantages, the nearby pastry kitchen adds to the monetary soundness of the local area, upholds neighborhood farming, and gives its clients new, top notch items, advancing capable utilization.

Moreover, private ventures frequently offer eco-accommodating items and administrations that line up with the standards of natural obligation. They figure out the rising significance of manageable and ecologically mindful practices and take care of the inclinations of clients who esteem these standards. Whether it's a store selling morally obtained clothing or a neighborhood café serving natural and privately developed food, independent ventures increase the value of the local area by giving supportable choices.

Moral practices and ecological obligation are characteristically connected. Private ventures that embrace moral direct frequently integrate natural obligation as a center component of their qualities. The two ideas complete one another, making an all encompassing way to deal with mindful business lead. This coordinated methodology cultivates a feeling of obligation that stretches out past benefit, empowering private companies to act to the greatest advantage of their networks and the climate.

Engaging independent companies to focus on moral practices and ecological obligation includes different aspects. Admittance to assets that help moral and eco-accommodating drives is fundamental, as it empowers private ventures to really carry out dependable practices.

Strengthening incorporates cultivating associations between independent ventures and associations that advance moral and maintainable works on, giving a stage to joint effort and information sharing that energizes capable direct.

Smoothing out guidelines to work with moral practices and ecological obligation is one more pivotal element of independent company strengthening. Decreasing regulatory deterrents and making consistence with moral and ecological guidelines more direct empowers private ventures to participate in capable strategic policies. The objective is to establish a climate where moral practices and natural obligation are empowered and upheld by government arrangements.

Tending to abberations in market power between private companies and bigger organizations is critical for enabling private ventures to embrace moral practices and natural obligation. Arrangements that advance fair contest and set out open doors for private companies to take on and advance mindful direct can even the odds. A decent commercial center guarantees that private ventures have the assets and impact to focus on moral and ecologically dependable practices.

Building a vigorous biological system of help is instrumental in private company strengthening for moral practices and natural obligation. Entrepreneurs can benefit extraordinarily from admittance to assets and stages that associate them with associations and specialists in moral and manageable strategic policies. These organizations give valuable open doors to private companies to find moral and eco-accommodating practices, participate in mindful business direct, and pursue informed decisions.

Encouraging a strong and comprehensive business climate is likewise of vital significance with regards to moral practices and ecological obligation. Perceiving the one of a kind commitments of private ventures and recognizing their job in nearby and worldwide economies can energize local area support, shopper commitment, and a better business environment that permits independent ventures to focus on moral and ecologically mindful direct.

The effect of engaging private ventures to embrace moral practices and ecological obligation reaches out a long ways past the singular level. At the point when independent ventures effectively embrace and advance moral and eco-accommodating practices, they make a chain response of advantages. These commitments not just upgrade the general personal satisfaction for nearby occupants yet additionally animate monetary turn of events and draw in additional interest nearby. Mindful business direct encourages a feeling of solidarity, shared values, and common trust, reinforcing the social texture and the climate.

Private ventures frequently partake in nearby occasions, support moral and natural drives, and backing magnanimous associations that attention on maintainability and capable strategic policies. These exercises assemble spans between private ventures and their networks, further reinforcing the bond.

At the point when private companies are effectively engaged with moral practices and ecological obligation, inhabitants are bound to help these ventures through their support, making a cooperative relationship that encourages dependable lead.

The feeling of spot and character encouraged by private ventures is instrumental in the reception and advancement of moral practices and ecological obligation. At the point when inhabitants have a special interaction with their nearby private ventures, they are bound to embrace moral lead and pursue ecologically mindful decisions. Independent companies act as center points for moral and natural instruction, where occupants shop as well as find out about mindful strategic approaches and maintainable utilization, reinforcing the social texture and the climate.

In a quickly changing worldwide scene, the idea of strengthening with regards to moral practices and ecological obligation isn't static. It develops because of arising difficulties and open doors. For instance, the computerized change has altogether modified the independent venture strengthening scene. The appearance of the web and internet business has opened up new roads for independent ventures to embrace and advance moral practices and natural obligation and arrive at a worldwide client base. Internet advertising and deals stages have permitted even the littlest endeavors to keep a web-based .

Chapter 5

Challenges and Opportunities

The way to engaging independent companies to embrace manageability, neighborhood obtaining, moral practices, and natural obligation is loaded down with the two difficulties and open doors. As these undertakings explore the mind boggling scene of business tasks and local area commitment, they experience different deterrents, while at the same time getting a charge out of interesting possibilities for development and positive effect. In this investigation, we dig into the diverse difficulties and potential open doors that characterize the excursion of private companies towards an additional supportable and moral future.

Challenges:

Monetary Requirements: Private ventures frequently face impediments in getting to the fundamental monetary assets to put resources into maintainability and dependable practices. Bigger organizations might have more significant financial plans and assets available to them, making it trying for private ventures to contend in a similar space.

Administrative Intricacy: The administrative scene can be multifaceted, with a bunch of rules and guidelines overseeing different parts of business lead, from natural guidelines to moral practices. Conforming to these guidelines can be a weight for private ventures, especially when they miss the mark on assets to explore complex legitimate structures.

Market Rivalry: Private ventures frequently battle with contest from bigger partnerships with greater promoting financial plans and memorability. It tends to be trying for more modest undertakings to convey the worth of their maintainable and moral practices to customers who are frequently immersed with publicizing from bigger firms.

Inventory network The board: While independent ventures frequently focus on neighborhood obtaining, overseeing supply chains effectively can be a test. Keeping up with predictable associations with neighborhood providers and guaranteeing moral obtaining rehearses call for investment and assets.

Shopper Mindfulness: Instructing purchasers about the significance of supportable and moral practices can be a daunting task. Private companies should put resources into showcasing and correspondence techniques to bring issues to light and stress their obligation to dependable lead.

Scaling Manageability: As independent companies develop, increasing supportability practices can be intricate. Keeping up with supportable tasks while growing and guaranteeing that similar standards are stuck to for a bigger scope can challenge.

Protection from Change: Changing laid out strategic approaches and embracing maintainability, nearby obtaining, and moral direct may confront obstruction from workers and the executives. Defeating this opposition and cultivating a culture of liability and supportability can challenge.

Open doors:

Local area Commitment: Private companies enjoy the one of a kind benefit of being profoundly implanted in their networks. This neighborhood presence gives chances to close commitment with local area individuals and associations, cultivating a feeling of shared liability and advancing manageability.

Adaptability and Flexibility: Private ventures are many times more nimble and versatile than bigger enterprises. This adaptability permits them to answer quickly to arising manageability patterns and buyer inclinations, offering eco-accommodating items and administrations that line up with evolving requests.

Purchaser Inclinations: Developing buyer interest in manageability, moral practices, and privately obtained items presents a huge chance for private companies. These ventures can take advantage of a market of cognizant customers who effectively look for dependable other options.

Computerized Change: The advanced upset has opened new roads for independent ventures to interface with buyers, providers, and accomplices. Online stages and web-based entertainment empower private companies to bring issues to light of their economical and moral practices on a worldwide scale.

Cooperative Drives: Independent companies can unite to advance manageability and capable practices. Cooperative endeavors, for example, nearby manageability organizations and business affiliations, empower little ventures to all in all use assets and information.

Government Backing: Government strategies and monetary help can establish an ideal climate for private companies focused on maintainability and moral practices. Alleviation projects and motivating forces can assist these endeavors with exploring difficulties and put resources into dependable lead.

Client Steadfastness: By effectively captivating in maintainability and moral practices, private ventures can areas of strength for cultivate dedication. Shoppers who line up with a business' qualities are bound to stay faithful clients, making a steady income base for these ventures.

Advancement: Independent ventures frequently act as center points of advancement, growing new methodologies and arrangements that can promote manageability objectives. Their dexterity and inventiveness empower them to investigate novel techniques for tending to ecological and moral difficulties.

The difficulties and potential open doors experienced by private companies in their excursion towards maintainability, neighborhood obtaining, moral practices, and ecological obligation highlight the unique idea of this pursuit. While challenges like monetary imperatives, administrative intricacy, and market rivalry request clever fixes, the open doors introduced by local area commitment, adaptability, and shopper inclinations offer the potential for development and positive effect. Engaging independent companies to embrace manageability requires a diverse methodology that use their exceptional assets and addresses the difficulties they face, at last adding to an additional feasible and moral future.

5.1 Overcoming Challenges Faced by Small Businesses

Private ventures, frequently described by their unobtrusive size and limited presence, assume a vital part in driving monetary development and cultivating local area prosperity. In any case, they face a scope of difficulties that can thwart their turn of events and maintainability. These difficulties incorporate restricted admittance to capital, rivalry from bigger companies, administrative intricacies, and the need to adjust to quickly changing economic situations. In this investigation, we dive into the complex difficulties looked by private ventures and consider procedures and answers for conquering these snags, guaranteeing their proceeded with progress and commitment to the nearby and worldwide economies.

Challenges:

Restricted Admittance to Capital: One of the essential difficulties looked by private companies is restricted admittance to capital. Getting supporting for tasks, development, and manageability drives can be a huge obstacle. Conventional banks frequently force severe measures and request insurance, making it hard for independent companies to get credits.

Market Contest: Private ventures frequently rival bigger organizations with greater assets and memorability. These bigger elements can rule markets and posture critical difficulties to the development and productivity of private companies.

Administrative Intricacy: The administrative climate can complex and request, with a huge number of rules and principles overseeing different parts of business tasks. Private companies might miss the mark on assets and ability expected to explore these guidelines successfully, bringing about consistence challenges.

Store network The board: Overseeing supply chains productively can be testing, especially when independent companies focus on nearby obtaining and moral practices. Reliably keeping up with associations with neighborhood providers and guaranteeing moral obtaining rehearses call for investment and assets.

Customer Mindfulness: Instructing shoppers about the significance of supportability, moral practices, and privately obtained items can be a considerable undertaking. Private companies need to put resources into advertising and correspondence techniques to bring issues to light and underscore their obligation to mindful direct.

Scaling Maintainability: As independent companies develop, increasing supportability practices can be mind boggling. Keeping up with reasonable tasks while growing and guaranteeing that similar standards are stuck to for a bigger scope can challenge.

Protection from Change: Changing laid out strategic policies and embracing supportability, nearby obtaining, and moral lead might confront obstruction from workers and the board. Defeating this obstruction and encouraging a culture of liability and supportability can be a significant test.

Techniques for Defeating Difficulties:

Broaden Wellsprings of Capital: Private ventures can defeat their capital constraints by enhancing their wellsprings of subsidizing. Past conventional bank advances, they can investigate elective choices like funding, private supporters, crowdfunding, and microloans. Every one of these funding techniques offers exceptional benefits, making it simpler for private companies to get the capital they need.

Embrace Computerized Change: Utilizing innovation and the advanced change can furnish independent ventures with an upper hand. They can lay out a web-based presence, arrive at a more extensive client base, and smooth out tasks through online business stages and computerized showcasing. Embracing innovation permits independent ventures to adjust to changing economic situations and answer shopper inclinations all the more really.

Cooperative Endeavors: Private ventures can frame partnerships and cooperative organizations to by and large handle difficulties. Neighborhood maintainability organizations and business affiliations permit little undertakings to pool their assets, share information, and backing each other in embracing reasonable and moral practices. Cooperative endeavors upgrade their aggregate effect and empower them to defeat market rivalry.

Smooth out Production network The executives: Independent ventures can improve production network the board by embracing current store network programming and innovation. These apparatuses assist with smoothing out acquirement, stock administration, and strategies, making it simpler for private companies to keep up with economical practices and effective nearby obtaining.

Advocate for Administrative Changes: Private ventures can take part in backing endeavors to advance administrative changes that are more strong of their requirements. By working with industry affiliations and government bodies, they can partake in conversations and drives pointed toward streamlining and working on the administrative climate. Administrative changes that decrease consistence weights can enable independent companies to flourish.

Instruction and Mindfulness: Raising shopper mindfulness about the worth of supportability, moral practices, and privately obtained items is a fundamental stage for independent companies. They can put resources into showcasing and advertising efforts that feature their obligation to these standards, teaching purchasers about the positive effect of their decisions.

Representative Preparation and Commitment: Conquering protection from change and encouraging a culture of liability and supportability inside the association requires worker preparing and commitment. Private ventures can carry out preparing programs that underline the significance of supportability and morals. Connecting with representatives in dynamic cycles and perceiving their commitments can additionally urge their obligation to these standards.

Open doors for Independent ventures:

While private ventures face a scope of difficulties, they likewise appreciate interesting open doors that can move their development and achievement. These open doors emerge from their limited presence, versatility, and the changing inclinations of shoppers and financial backers.

Local area Commitment: Private companies are well established in their networks. They can effectively draw in with local area individuals, construct trust, and encourage a feeling of shared liability. This commitment gives potential open doors to private ventures to acquire nearby help and advance supportability drives that line up with local area values.

Adaptability and Flexibility: Private ventures are many times more light-footed and versatile than bigger organizations. Their adaptability permits them to answer quickly to arising manageability drifts and changing buyer inclinations. Independent ventures can use their versatility to offer eco-accommodating items and administrations that line up with developing requests.

Purchaser Inclinations: The rising interest in manageability, moral practices, and privately obtained items presents a huge chance for private ventures. They can take care of a developing business sector of cognizant customers effectively looking for capable other options.

By adjusting their contributions to purchaser inclinations, private companies can draw in and hold a steadfast client base.

Advanced Change: The computerized unrest has opened new roads for private ventures to associate with purchasers, providers, and accomplices. Online stages and virtual entertainment empower private ventures to bring issues to light of their economical and moral practices on a worldwide scale. The advanced change engages private companies to contend really in the cutting edge commercial center.

Government Backing: Government strategies and monetary help can establish a great climate for private ventures focused on manageability and moral practices. Alleviation projects and impetuses can assist these ventures with exploring difficulties and put resources into capable direct. By teaming up with government bodies, independent companies can impact arrangements that work with their development and supportability.

Client Dedication: By effectively captivating in maintainability and moral practices, private ventures can serious areas of strength for encourage unwaveringness. Shoppers who line up with a business' qualities are bound to stay steadfast clients, making a steady income base for these ventures.

Advancement: Independent ventures frequently act as center points of advancement, growing new methodologies and arrangements that can promote maintainability objectives. Their nimbleness and inventiveness empower them to investigate novel strategies for tending to natural and moral difficulties. By embracing advancement, private companies can bear outing in their business sectors and add to the improvement of practical arrangements.

5.2 Identifying Opportunities for Growth and Development

Independent ventures, frequently hailed as the foundation of nearby and public economies, are strategically set up to recognize and take advantage of chances for development and improvement. Their exceptional qualities, like limited presence, flexibility, and solid local area associations, furnish them with particular benefits in perceiving and profiting by valuable open doors. In this investigation, we dive into the techniques and approaches that engage private ventures to distinguish, saddle, and influence valuable open doors for development and improvement, guaranteeing their proceeded with progress and commitment to the monetary scene.

Techniques for Distinguishing Valuable open doors:

Statistical surveying and Investigation: Independent ventures can start by leading intensive statistical surveying and examination to recognize holes, drifts, and arising client needs. This examination assists them with acquiring bits of knowledge into their objective market and permits them to in like manner change their contributions.

Client Criticism: Paying attention to client input is an important system for distinguishing open doors. Clients frequently give bits of knowledge into their inclinations, concerns, and neglected needs. Independent companies can effectively look for and influence this input to refine their items, administrations, and tasks.

Contender Investigation: It is critical to Figure out the serious scene. By investigating their rivals, independent companies can distinguish regions where they can separate themselves and proposition exceptional worth to their clients. This investigation empowers them to jump all over market chances and reinforce their cutthroat position.

Versatility: The adaptability and flexibility inborn to private ventures permit them to turn rapidly in light of evolving conditions. By remaining deft and receptive to advertise shifts, independent companies can distinguish and immediately take advantage of chances that bigger partnerships could ignore.

Systems administration and Organizations: Building an organization of industry contacts and shaping vital organizations can open ways to new open doors. These connections can give experiences, references, and cooperative endeavors that encourage development and improvement.

Advancement and Innovativeness: Empowering development and inventive reasoning inside the association can prompt the distinguishing proof of new open doors. Private companies ought to establish a climate that upholds thought age and critical thinking, as this can reveal novel ways for development.

Approaches for Quickly jumping all over Chances:

Enhancement: Private ventures can immediately take advantage of chances for development by broadening their contributions. Extending product offerings or administrations permits them to take advantage of new business sectors and client portions, diminishing the gamble related with over-dependence on a solitary item or administration.

Nearby Commitment: Utilizing their restricted presence, private ventures can effectively draw in with their networks. They can support neighborhood occasions, partake in local area drives, and backing beneficent associations. These exercises advance generosity as well as entryways to possible organizations and valuable learning experiences.

Online Presence: In an undeniably advanced world, laying out and it is imperative to keep a web-based presence. Private ventures can use sites, virtual entertainment, and online business stages to arrive at a more extensive client base and grow their market reach. This computerized change empowers them to take advantage of a worldwide crowd.

Client Maintenance: Perceiving the benefit of existing clients, independent companies can zero in on client maintenance. Faithful clients are bound to return and allude others, filling in as diplomats for the business. Offering incredible client assistance and devotion projects can encourage development through client backing.

Functional Productivity: Upgrading inward tasks can prompt expense reserve funds and proficiency enhancements. By smoothing out processes, decreasing waste, and improving efficiency, private companies can let loose assets to put resources into development drives.

Vital Coalitions: Teaming up with different organizations or associations can give admittance to new business sectors and assets. Vital coalitions, joint endeavors, and organizations empower independent companies to use corresponding qualities and jump all over development chances.

Product and Global Extension: Private ventures can investigate worldwide business sectors to extend their client base. Sending out items or administrations to unfamiliar business sectors can open up new learning experiences. Taxpayer supported initiatives and motivations frequently support private companies in their worldwide extension endeavors.

Embracing Advancement and Innovation:

The coordination of innovation and development is instrumental in distinguishing and taking advantage of development chances. Private companies can tackle the force of computerized instruments and information examination to pursue informed choices and stay cutthroat. Putting resources into innovation can empower independent companies to smooth out tasks, contact more extensive crowds, and further develop client encounters.

Internet business: The ascent of internet business stages has changed the retail scene. Private ventures can make online stores to arrive at clients past their nearby geological region. Web based business gives chances to expanded deals, worldwide reach, and enhanced income streams.

Information Investigation: Dissecting information can uncover significant bits of knowledge into client conduct and market patterns. Private companies can utilize information examination to tailor their items and promoting methodologies to line up with client inclinations and immediately jump all over development chances.

Robotization: The mechanization of routine errands can save time and assets for additional essential undertakings. Independent ventures can carry out robotization for assignments like stock administration, client support, and promoting, permitting them to zero in on distinguishing and exploiting learning experiences.

Man-made reasoning: simulated intelligence controlled apparatuses can give private ventures prescient investigation and customized client encounters. By saddling man-made intelligence, independent companies can go with information driven choices and proposition improved administrations to their clients.

Computerized Showcasing: Internet publicizing and web-based entertainment promoting are amazing assets for contacting a more extensive crowd. Private companies can utilize advanced showcasing to increment brand perceivability, draw in new clients, and advance their items or administrations actually.

Distributed computing: Cloud-based arrangements empower independent companies to get to and oversee information, applications, and assets all the more proficiently. This innovation can upgrade cooperation, versatility, and availability, giving the establishment to development.

5.3 The Economic Resilience of Small Businesses

The monetary scene is set apart by consistent change, developing difficulties, and unanticipated interruptions. Even with monetary slumps, worldwide emergencies, and mechanical unrests, the versatility of independent ventures arises as an essential determinant of financial steadiness and development. Private ventures, portrayed by their unassuming size and limited presence, show exceptional attributes that make them tough in the midst of difficulty. In this investigation, we dig into the purposes for the financial versatility of private companies, the procedures that empower them to climate monetary tempests, and their vital job in cultivating local area prosperity and supported monetary turn of events.

Why Private ventures Are Monetarily Versatile:

Adaptability and Flexibility: Private ventures are known for their nimbleness and versatility. Their size permits them to turn rapidly because of evolving conditions, like changes in customer inclinations or financial slumps. This versatility empowers private companies to stay deft and change their systems to get by and flourish in unique monetary circumstances.

Limited Presence: Private companies are well established in their neighborhood networks. This limited presence furnishes them with a steady client base and steadfast customers, in any event, during testing monetary times. Local area support assumes a huge part in the financial versatility of private ventures, as occupants frequently lift up these undertakings during difficulty.

Solid Client Connections: Private ventures focus on major areas of strength for building enduring associations with their clients. These connections encourage unwaveringness, rehash business, and verbal exchange references. During financial slumps, the trust and unique interactions between private companies and their clients can be a life saver, assisting these endeavors with enduring the hardship.

Specialty Markets and Specialization: Numerous private ventures work in specialty advertises or have practical experience specifically items or administrations. This specialization frequently permits them to keep a devoted client base, even despite more extensive financial difficulties. Private companies that take care of explicit requirements and inclinations are bound to hold their clients during monetary slumps.

Lower Working Expenses: Independent ventures ordinarily have lower working expenses contrasted with bigger enterprises. They can smooth out their activities, decrease above costs, and work effectively. This cost-effectiveness adds to their monetary flexibility, as it permits them to work beneficially, even in testing financial circumstances.

Local area Commitment: Private companies effectively draw in with their neighborhood networks. This commitment cultivates client unwaveringness as well as opens ways to local area support during extreme monetary times. Occupants frequently perceive the worth of private ventures in their networks and will uphold them when confronted with monetary difficulties.

Systems for Financial Versatility:

Expand Income Streams: Independent companies can upgrade their monetary versatility by differentiating their wellsprings of income. Offering a scope of items or administrations, venturing into related markets, or taking advantage of reciprocal revenue streams can give security during monetary variances.

Backup stash and Monetary Preparation: Building a rainy day account and rehearsing sound monetary arranging are crucial techniques for financial flexibility. Private companies ought to save a piece of their benefits as a monetary pad to cover surprising costs or times of diminished income. Monetary arranging guarantees that assets are overseen effectively.

Statistical surveying and Transformation: Ceaselessly observing business sector patterns and client inclinations permits private ventures to adjust rapidly to evolving conditions. They can change their contributions, evaluating, and promoting techniques because of financial difficulties and arising open doors.

Cost Control and Effectiveness: Independent companies ought to zero in on controlling expenses and improving functional productivity. Smoothing out processes, lessening waste, and arranging great terms with providers can bring down working costs, adding to financial strength.

Online Presence and Web based business: Laying out a strong web-based presence and utilizing online business stages can grow market reach and give an extra income stream. The capacity to arrive at clients past the neighborhood online deals is particularly significant during monetary interruptions.

Client Maintenance and Devotion: Focusing on client maintenance through outstanding assistance and unwaveringness projects can support monetary versatility. Steadfast clients are bound to keep supporting independent companies during testing times and allude others, prompting supported income.

Risk The executives and Possibility Arranging: Fostering a gamble the board technique and alternate course of action is fundamental. Independent ventures ought to recognize possible dangers and make intends to relieve them. Readiness can limit the effect of unexpected disturbances on their financial security.

Cooperative Drives: Teaming up with other private ventures, industry affiliations, and local area associations can improve monetary strength. Associations can give admittance to assets, shared information, and aggregate help during monetary difficulties.

The Job of Private companies in Monetary Flexibility:
Independent ventures are monetarily versatile substances as well as indispensable parts of a tough economy. Their commitments stretch out past their own monetary endurance and thriving to the more extensive prosperity of networks and the generally financial soundness of locales and countries.

Neighborhood Financial Solidness: Private ventures are fundamental supporters of nearby monetary steadiness. They give work open doors, invigorate shopper spending, and backing neighborhood providers. During monetary slumps, their capacity to keep up with tasks and hold representatives settles networks and forestall further financial downfall.

Work Creation: Independent ventures are critical work makers. They enlist locally, cultivating business open doors and lessening joblessness rates. At the point when the economy faces difficulties, the job of private companies in work creation turns out to be significantly more basic, as they can assist with engrossing dislodged laborers from bigger partnerships.

Advancement and Strength Culture: Private companies frequently act as center points of development. Their flexibility, inventiveness, and enterprising soul urge creative answers for financial difficulties. Moreover, they encourage a culture of flexibility and diligence, motivating others to beat difficulty.

Local area Prosperity: Private companies assume a focal part in cultivating local area prosperity. Their commitment with neighborhood inhabitants, sponsorship of local area occasions, and backing for beneficent associations reinforce the social texture. During financial hardships, this feeling of local area can inspire spirits and add to close to home versatility.

Monetary Variety: Independent ventures add to financial variety by offering a wide cluster of items and administrations. This variety upgrades financial flexibility by decreasing reliance on a solitary industry or market area. It guarantees that networks are not excessively helpless against financial shocks in unambiguous areas.

Business and Financial Development: Independent ventures are many times the origin of business. They support groundbreaking thoughts and adventures, which can develop into huge monetary benefactors. The outcome of private companies today frequently establishes the groundwork for the development and improvement of bigger undertakings later on.

Worldwide Intensity: Private ventures that embrace financial flexibility procedures can turn out to be universally serious. By utilizing their limited assets, adaptability, and development, they can venture into worldwide business sectors and add to a country's monetary seriousness on a worldwide scale.

Difficulties to Monetary Strength:

In spite of their one of a kind benefits and commitments, private ventures likewise face difficulties that can test their monetary versatility. These difficulties incorporate restricted admittance to capital, contest from bigger partnerships, administrative intricacies, and the need to adjust to quickly changing economic situations.

Restricted Admittance to Capital: Getting supporting for tasks, development, and financial strength drives can be trying for private companies. Conventional banks frequently force severe models and request insurance, making it challenging for these ventures to get to the capital they need.

Market Rivalry: Independent companies frequently battle with contest from bigger partnerships with greater assets and memorability. These bigger elements can overwhelm markets and posture critical difficulties to the development and productivity of independent ventures.

Administrative Intricacy: The administrative climate can be complicated, with a heap of rules and guidelines overseeing different parts of business tasks. Conforming to these guidelines can be a weight for independent ventures, especially when they miss the mark on assets to explore complex lawful structures.

Store network The executives: Overseeing supply chains effectively can be testing, especially when private companies focus on nearby obtaining and moral practices. Keeping up with predictable associations with nearby providers and guaranteeing moral obtaining rehearses call for investment and assets.

Chapter 6

Strategies to Support Small Businesses

Supporting independent companies is urgent for monetary development and local area improvement. These undertakings assume a huge part in work creation, development, and cultivating nearby business. Nonetheless, private ventures frequently face special difficulties that can block their prosperity. To address these difficulties and offer successful help for independent ventures, a complex methodology is fundamental. This article will investigate different techniques to help private ventures, including admittance to capital, business schooling and preparing, administrative change, computerized change, and local area commitment.

Admittance to capital is a basic calculate the progress of independent companies. Numerous entrepreneurs battle to get supporting, which can be a hindrance to development and maintainability. One system to help private ventures in such manner is to furnish them with more noteworthy admittance to capital through credits, awards, and speculation programs. Monetary organizations, both customary and elective loan specialists, can assume a critical part in this work. They can fit their loaning items to meet the particular necessities of independent companies, offering adaptable reimbursement terms and lower financing costs.

Government offices can likewise add to independent company capital help by making programs that give credit ensures, awards, or appropriations to qualified organizations. These drives can assist with lessening the monetary gamble for moneylenders and urge them to stretch out credit to little undertakings. Also, private backers, investors, and crowdfunding stages can give value capital, permitting independent ventures to raise assets for extension, item advancement, or development. Cooperative endeavors among different partners, including government offices, monetary organizations, and financial backers, can make a vigorous environment for private venture funding.

As well as giving admittance to capital, private companies benefit from designated business instruction and preparing programs. These projects outfit business visionaries with the information and abilities expected to actually oversee and develop their organizations. Entrepreneurs might miss the mark on administration and monetary abilities, blocking their capacity to pursue educated choices and explore the intricacies regarding running an organization. To address this, support associations can offer studios, instructional meetings, and online seminars on points like monetary administration, promoting, and HR. In addition, mentorship projects can associate experienced business experts with entrepreneurs, giving significant direction and guidance.

Government offices and industry affiliations can assume a urgent part in planning and financing these schooling and preparing programs. These drives can take care of the particular requirements of private ventures, assisting them with adjusting to changing economic situations and stay serious. Generally speaking, these projects can prompt superior business execution, expanded productivity, and upgraded work creation. Empowering deep rooted learning among entrepreneurs and their representatives can additionally add to the achievement and versatility of these undertakings.

Administrative change is one more fundamental procedure to help independent ventures. Numerous entrepreneurs wrestle with intricate and oppressive guidelines that can smother development and advancement. Smoothing out and improving on administrative cycles can establish a better climate for independent companies to flourish. Government organizations ought to work cooperatively with business relationship to distinguish and address administrative difficulties that lopsidedly influence little undertakings. By lessening administrative noise and consistence costs, organizations can designate assets all the more proficiently and center around their center exercises.

Besides, charge strategies can fundamentally affect independent ventures. Charge impetuses and credits planned explicitly for little undertakings can assist with lessening their monetary weight and support speculation. Tax cuts for innovative work, recruiting, and capital venture can be especially powerful in supporting private companies. Improving on the expense code and limiting the authoritative weight of duty consistence can likewise save time and assets for entrepreneurs.

Advanced change is turning out to be progressively significant for private ventures to remain cutthroat in the present innovation driven world. Embracing advanced apparatuses and innovations can upgrade efficiency, arrive at new business sectors, and further develop client commitment. To help private companies in their advanced excursion, legislatures, industry affiliations, and innovation suppliers can team up to offer preparation and assets. These can help entrepreneurs comprehend and embrace computerized advances that are applicable to their industry and plan of action.

Internet business stages, site advancement, and computerized advertising are regions where private companies can profit from designated help. Web based business empowers independent ventures to arrive at a worldwide client base, while a solid internet based presence can further develop brand perceivability and client securing. Network safety is likewise basic as private ventures can be powerless against cyberattacks. In this manner, preparing programs that cover computerized security and information assurance are vital for shield business tasks and client data.

Local area commitment is a frequently misjudged yet imperative technique to help private ventures. A solid feeling of local area can encourage a strong climate for nearby organizations and advance a "shop neighborhood" culture. Nearby legislatures, offices of trade, and local area associations can assume a huge part in making a flourishing business environment. They can arrange occasions, like ranchers' business sectors, nearby celebrations, and neighborhood clean-ups, to unite the local area and advance private ventures.

Cooperation among neighborhood organizations is likewise fundamental. Private companies can accomplice to send off joint showcasing efforts, reliability projects, and local area drives. Empowering occupants to help their nearby organizations by purchasing neighborhood can assist with making a reasonable client base for little endeavors. Besides, public acquirement strategies that favor neighborhood providers can animate monetary development at the local area level.

Taking everything into account, supporting private ventures is fundamental for monetary development and local area improvement. Admittance to capital, business instruction and preparing, administrative change, advanced change, and local area commitment are key methodologies to engage independent companies. Giving little endeavors the monetary assets they need, furnishing them with the information and abilities to succeed, improving on guidelines, advancing computerized reception, and encouraging a feeling of local area can all add to the achievement and maintainability of independent ventures. A comprehensive methodology that includes government offices, monetary organizations, industry affiliations, and nearby networks is impor-tant to establish a helpful climate for private companies to prosper.

Independent ventures are the foundation of numerous economies, giving business open doors, driving advancement, and adding to the variety and energy of networks. Nonetheless, they frequently face difficulties that can ruin their development and manageability. To address these difficulties and offer successful help for private ven-tures, a multi-layered approach is fundamental. This article will investigate different techniques to help private ventures, including admittance to capital, business in-struction and preparing, administrative change, computerized change, and local area commitment.

Admittance to capital is a basic figure the progress of independent companies. Numerous entrepreneurs battle to get funding, which can be a hindrance to develop-ment and supportability.

One methodology to help private ventures in such manner is to furnish them with more noteworthy admittance to capital through credits, awards, and speculation programs. Monetary organizations, both customary and elective loan specialists, can assume a critical part in this work. They can fit their loaning items to meet the particular necessities of independent companies, offering adaptable reimbursement terms and lower financing costs.

Government offices can likewise add to independent venture capital help by making programs that give advance ensures, awards, or appropriations to qualified organizations. These drives can assist with decreasing the monetary gamble for moneylenders and urge them to stretch out credit to little undertakings. Moreover, private supporters, investors, and crowdfunding stages can give value capital, permitting independent ventures to raise assets for extension, item improvement, or advancement. Cooperative endeavors among different partners, including government organizations, monetary foundations, and financial backers, can make a strong environment for independent company funding.

As well as giving admittance to capital, private companies benefit from designated business instruction and preparing programs. These projects outfit business people with the information and abilities expected to really oversee and develop their organizations. Entrepreneurs might miss the mark on administration and monetary abilities, obstructing their capacity to settle on educated choices and explore the intricacies regarding running an organization. To address this, support associations can offer studios, instructional meetings, and online seminars on subjects like monetary administration, showcasing, and HR. Additionally, mentorship projects can interface experienced business experts with entrepreneurs, giving important direction and guidance.

6.1 Buying Local: The Power of Consumer Choices

Shopper decisions significantly affect the economy, the climate, and the prosperity of networks. At the point when shoppers decide to purchase neighborhood items and backing independent ventures, they add to different positive results. Purchasing nearby fortifies neighborhood economies as well as lessens natural effect, advances local area improvement, and encourages a feeling of association among makers and buyers. In this article, we will investigate the force of shopper decisions in supporting neighborhood organizations, talking about the monetary, natural, and social advantages of purchasing nearby.

Neighborhood organizations are the backbone of networks, giving position, merchandise, and administrations that meet the one of a kind necessities of occupants. At the point when buyers decide to spend their cash at neighborhood organizations, they keep a more critical part of their dollars inside the local area. Dissimilar to enormous organizations with base camp in far off urban communities, neighborhood organizations tend to reinvest a more significant piece of their profit in the nearby economy. This reinvestment upholds work creation, business development, and local area advancement.

Also, purchasing nearby diminishes pay imbalance. In numerous networks, entrepreneurs are bound to reside in similar region where they work their organizations. At the point when shoppers support nearby organizations, they add to the monetary prosperity of their neighbors, companions, and individual local area individuals. This, thusly, can prompt expanded monetary strength and thriving for a more extensive fragment of the populace.

Conversely, when purchasers principally belittle huge, global companies, a critical part of the cash spent leaves the neighborhood economy. These companies might be settled far away, and their benefits frequently go to investors who might have no association with the local area where the items or administrations are bought. The progression of cash out of the local area can prompt monetary stagnation and decreased open doors for inhabitants.

Nearby organizations likewise assume an imperative part in forming the person and character of networks. They give special items and administrations that mirror the nearby culture, history, and values. From high quality specialties to family-claimed cafés, these organizations add a particular flavor to the local area that can't be imitated by mainstream stores. The presence of neighborhood organizations makes a feeling of spot and having a place, which is fundamental for encouraging areas of strength for a personality.

Moreover, neighborhood organizations frequently take part in magnanimous exercises, supporting nearby foundations, schools, and local area occasions. They are bound to support nearby games groups, give to neighborhood causes, and partake in local area improvement projects. This sort of local area commitment can decidedly affect the general prosperity of occupants and add to a dynamic and strong local area.

At the point when shoppers decide to purchase nearby, they additionally assist with decreasing the ecological impression related with transportation and supply chains. Neighborhood organizations will more often than not source their items and materials from adjacent providers, decreasing the requirement for significant distance delivery and transportation. This outcomes in less ozone harming substance discharges and a lower ecological effect. Interestingly, enormous worldwide partnerships frequently depend on worldwide inventory chains, which can prompt critical fossil fuel byproducts, contamination, and asset consumption.

Besides, neighborhood organizations are bound to participate in reasonable and naturally capable practices. Limited scope makers and ranchers frequently focus on eco-accommodating strategies, for example, natural cultivating and manageable creation methods, which can assist with safeguarding nearby environments and decrease the utilization of hurtful synthetic compounds. Neighborhood organizations arc likewise more associated with the networks they serve and are, subsequently, more spurred to safeguard nearby regular assets and scenes.

Purchasing neighborhood can prompt a more supportable and tough food framework. Neighborhood food creation and dissemination frameworks diminish the distance food makes a trip from homestead to table.

This diminishes the ecological effect as well as expands the newness and healthy benefit of the food. By supporting neighborhood ranchers and food makers, purchasers can assist with safeguarding nearby food customs and guarantee that food creation stays a reasonable occupation in their networks.

Notwithstanding the monetary and ecological advantages, purchasing neighborhood can cultivate a feeling of local area and association among makers and buyers. At the point when customers purchase from nearby organizations, they frequently have the chance to meet individuals behind the items. This special interaction can prompt a seriously enhancing shopping experience, as buyers can find out about the items they buy and the tales of individuals who make them.

Neighborhood organizations frequently invest wholeheartedly in their items and administrations, and they are bound to give customized client care. This makes a feeling of trust and dependability among customers and organizations, prompting durable and commonly valuable connections. Independent companies depend on recurrent clients, and they frequently put in any amount of work to guarantee consumer loyalty.

Also, purchasing neighborhood can prompt expanded straightforwardness in the production network. Shoppers are bound to know where their items come from and how they are made when they purchase from neighborhood organizations. This straightforwardness can be particularly urgent with regards to food items, as customers progressively look for data about the starting points and creation strategies for the things they devour.

Buyer decisions have the ability to shape the predetermination of neighborhood organizations and networks. At the point when customers decide to purchase nearby, they add to the monetary imperativeness of their networks, support work creation, lessen ecological effect, advance local area improvement, and encourage a feeling of association among makers and shoppers. By perceiving the significant effect of their decisions, customers can have a constructive outcome in their nearby and worldwide networks.

Nearby organizations are the soul of networks, giving position, products, and administrations that meet the extraordinary necessities of occupants. At the point when customers decide to spend their cash at nearby organizations, they keep a more huge part of their dollars inside the local area. Not at all like enormous partnerships with central command in far off urban communities, nearby organizations tend to reinvest a more significant piece of their profit in the neighborhood economy. This reinvestment upholds work creation, business development, and local area advancement.

In addition, purchasing neighborhood lessens pay imbalance. In numerous networks, entrepreneurs are bound to reside in similar region where they work their organizations.

At the point when customers support nearby organizations, they add to the financial prosperity of their neighbors, companions, and individual local area individuals. This, thusly, can prompt expanded financial solidness and thriving for a more extensive portion of the populace.

Interestingly, when shoppers basically disparage enormous, global enterprises, a critical piece of the cash spent leaves the nearby economy. These partnerships might be settled far away, and their benefits frequently go to investors who might have no association with the local area where the items or administrations are bought. The progression of cash out of the local area can prompt monetary stagnation and diminished open doors for occupants.

Neighborhood organizations likewise assume an imperative part in forming the person and character of networks. They give one of a kind items and administrations that mirror the neighborhood culture, history, and values. From high quality specialties to family-possessed cafés, these organizations add an unmistakable flavor to the local area that can't be duplicated by popular stores. The presence of neighborhood organizations makes a feeling of spot and having a place, which is fundamental for encouraging areas of strength for a personality.

Moreover, neighborhood organizations frequently take part in generous exercises, supporting nearby causes, schools, and local area occasions. They are bound to support nearby games groups, give to neighborhood causes, and partake in local area improvement projects. This sort of local area commitment can emphatically affect the general prosperity of inhabitants and add to a lively and durable local area.

At the point when shoppers decide to purchase nearby, they likewise assist with lessening the natural impression related with transportation and supply chains. Neighborhood organizations will generally source their items and materials from adjacent providers, diminishing the requirement for significant distance delivery and transportation. This outcomes in less ozone depleting substance emanations and a lower ecological effect. Interestingly, enormous worldwide partnerships frequently depend on worldwide stock chains, which can prompt critical fossil fuel byproducts, contamination, and asset exhaustion.

Besides, neighborhood organizations are bound to take part in supportable and ecologically mindful practices. Limited scope makers and ranchers frequently focus on eco-accommodating strategies, for example, natural cultivating and feasible creation procedures, which can assist with safeguarding neighborhood biological systems and lessen the utilization of hurtful synthetic substances. Nearby organizations are likewise more associated with the networks they serve and are, hence, more spurred to safeguard neighborhood regular assets and scenes.

Purchasing neighborhood can prompt a more supportable and versatile food framework. Neighborhood food creation and dispersion frameworks lessen the distance food ventures out from ranch to table. This diminishes the natural effect as well as builds the newness and healthy benefit of the food.

By supporting nearby ranchers and food makers, shoppers can assist with saving neighborhood food customs and guarantee that food creation stays a feasible business in their networks.

6.2 Promoting Awareness of Local Businesses

Advancing familiarity with nearby organizations is essential for their development and achievement. Little and nearby organizations are the foundation of numerous networks, adding to financial turn of events and giving interesting items and administrations. Be that as it may, in a world overwhelmed by enormous partnerships and online commercial centers, these neighborhood endeavors frequently battle to acquire perceivability and contend really. To assist neighborhood organizations with flourishing, crucial for carry out techniques increment mindfulness, support their advertising endeavors, and urge purchasers to pursue informed decisions that benefit their networks.

One compelling methodology for advancing attention to neighborhood organizations is to use the force of computerized showcasing and online stages. The web has turned into an essential wellspring of data for shoppers looking for items and administrations. Nearby organizations can make and keep serious areas of strength for a presence by creating easy to use sites, improving their substance for web crawlers, and drawing in with expected clients via online entertainment stages.

Having an appealing and enlightening site is essential for nearby organizations. It fills in as a virtual retail facade that permits likely clients to find out about the business, its contributions, and its area. Neighborhood organizations ought to guarantee their sites are versatile responsive, as a rising number of shoppers use cell phones to look for nearby items and administrations.

Website improvement (Web optimization) is one more basic part of online perceivability. Neighborhood organizations can streamline their site content to rank higher in web crawler results for pertinent watchwords. Also, they can guarantee their Google My Professional resource, which assists their business with showing up in neighborhood list items and on Google Guides.

Virtual entertainment is a significant instrument for building mindfulness and drawing in with the nearby local area. Nearby organizations can make and keep up with dynamic profiles on well known stages like Facebook, Instagram, and Twitter. Consistently posting content, cooperating with supporters, and running designated publicizing efforts can assist with expanding their perceivability and attract more clients to their physical or online customer facing facades.

One more way to deal with advancing attention to nearby organizations is to team up with neighborhood powerhouses and bloggers. These people have laid out followings and can assist nearby organizations with contacting a more extensive crowd.

Powerhouses and bloggers can visit the business, compose surveys, make connecting with content, and offer their encounters via virtual entertainment and their sites. Such coordinated efforts can create positive buzz and draw in new clients.

Besides, nearby organizations can profit from partaking in local area occasions and teaming up with other neighborhood organizations. Local area occasions, for example, road fairs, ranchers' business sectors, and celebrations, give fantastic open doors to organizations to exhibit their items and interface with potential clients eye to eye.

These occasions assist with making areas of strength for an of local area and advance neighborhood items and administrations.

Neighborhood organizations can likewise consider framing business affiliations or organizations with other little ventures in their space. By cooperating, they can cross-advance each other's items and administrations, which can be especially viable while focusing on a particular client segment. For example, a neighborhood bread kitchen and a café could team up to offer extraordinary advancements that urge clients to visit the two foundations.

Notwithstanding computerized advertising and local area commitment, customary showcasing strategies can in any case be powerful in advancing attention to neighborhood organizations. Regular postal mail missions, flyers, and handouts can be circulated inside the nearby local area to illuminate occupants about the organizations in their space. Neighborhood radio and papers may likewise offer publicizing valuable open doors that contact a nearby crowd successfully.

Support from nearby news sources can be significant in advancing familiarity with neighborhood organizations. Private ventures can contact neighborhood papers, magazines, radio broadcasts, and TV slots to share their accounts, achievements, and novel angles. Numerous neighborhood news sources are keen on highlighting nearby examples of overcoming adversity, and such inclusion can fundamentally help a business' perceivability and notoriety.

Advertising endeavors are one more methodology that nearby organizations can use to advance mindfulness. Making and conveying official statements about remarkable occasions, accomplishments, or local area inclusion can prompt media inclusion and expanded perceivability. Advertising likewise include building associations with columnists and powerhouses locally.

Local area commitment assumes a crucial part in advancing consciousness of neighborhood organizations. By effectively taking part in local area occasions, supporting neighborhood sports groups, or supporting magnanimous associations, nearby organizations can show their obligation to the local area's prosperity. Such endeavors add to positive brand picture as well as upgrade client devotion.

Besides, verbal exchange promoting stays an amazing asset for neighborhood organizations. Fulfilled clients who share their positive encounters with loved ones can become important brand advocates. Neighborhood organizations can empower and work with verbal exchange advertising by giving remarkable client care, requesting audits and references, and offering dependability projects or motivators for clients who acquire new business.

Neighborhood organizations can likewise consider facilitating their occasions, studios, or classes connected with their items or administrations. These occasions can draw in a nearby crowd and give an open door to organizations to exhibit their mastery, construct associations with clients, and advance their contributions.

In the present computerized age, online surveys and evaluations hold critical impact over customer choices. Neighborhood organizations ought to effectively deal with their web-based standing by empowering fulfilled clients to leave positive audits on stages like Google, Cry, or TripAdvisor. Furthermore, tending to negative surveys and settling client worries in an expert and straightforward way can show a guarantee to consumer loyalty.

Coordinated effort with nearby schools and instructive organizations can likewise be a significant system for advancing consciousness of neighborhood organizations. Nearby organizations can draw in with schools to give instructive encounters to understudies, whether through temporary jobs, visitor talks, or visits. This assists organizations with interfacing with the local area as well as constructs a pipeline of expected future representatives and clients.

Neighborhood organizations can likewise investigate associations with non-benefit associations and noble cause. Supporting nearby makes and drives exhibits a responsibility the local area's prosperity and can draw in clients who focus on working with socially mindful endeavors. Cooperative endeavors can go from raising support occasions to sponsorship amazing open doors.

6.3 Streamlining Regulations and Bureaucratic Hurdles

Smoothing out guidelines and regulatory obstacles is a basic part of encouraging monetary development, advancement, and effectiveness. Unnecessary guidelines and regulatory administrative noise can smother business advancement, deter business, and obstruct in general financial advancement. In this article, we will investigate the significance of rearranging and legitimizing guidelines, the difficulties in question, and the advantages that can be acknowledged by smoothing out regulatory cycles at nearby, territorial, and public levels.

To start, it's critical to recognize that guidelines fill a significant need in the public eye. They are intended to safeguard general wellbeing and security, guarantee fair contest, and address natural worries. Nonetheless, likewise with any framework, there is a fine equilibrium to be kept up with. Excessively difficult guidelines and regulatory strategies can make obstructions for organizations, especially little and medium-sized ventures (SMEs), and can prompt failures that thwart financial development.

One critical test in smoothing out guidelines is distinguishing which guidelines are over the top or pointless. Administrative structures frequently amass after some time as legislatures answer different issues and concerns. It very well may be trying to recognize guidelines that are really gainful and those that have outlasted their helpfulness. To address this test, administrative effect appraisals and intermittent surveys are fundamental. State run administrations ought to routinely assess existing guidelines, looking for input from organizations and partners to recognize decides that are old or excessively oppressive.

Straightforwardness is a critical component in this cycle. Legislatures ought to give clear data about existing guidelines and their effect, making it simpler for organizations to comprehend and follow the principles. Furthermore, including partners in the administrative survey process guarantees that a wide scope of viewpoints is thought of, which can prompt more compelling and designated administrative change.

The intricacy and irregularity of guidelines at various degrees of government can likewise introduce difficulties. In numerous nations, guidelines are laid out at the public level as well as at territorial and neighborhood levels. This can make an interwoven of decides and necessities that shift starting with one purview then onto the next. For organizations that work in numerous areas, consistence turns into a tangled and exorbitant cycle.

To resolve this issue, legislatures can attempt to fit guidelines across various degrees of government. This includes organizing endeavors to adjust rules and guidelines, making it simpler for organizations to explore administrative necessities in various locales. Harmonization endeavors can work on consistence and lessen the authoritative weight on organizations, especially SMEs that might miss the mark on assets to explore complex administrative scenes.

Moreover, the digitization of administrative cycles can significantly improve productivity and decrease regulatory obstacles. Moving towards e-government and advanced stages can work on associations among organizations and government offices. For instance, organizations can apply for grants, licenses, and other administrative endorsements web based, decreasing the requirement for actual desk work and in-person visits to government workplaces.

Advanced stages can likewise empower better coordination between various government divisions and organizations. For example, a solitary computerized entryway can act as an all in one resource for organizations to get to data, submit applications, and track the advancement of administrative cycles. This smoothes out communications with the public authority and decreases the authoritative weight on the two organizations and local officials.

Additionally, the utilization of innovation, for example, man-made reasoning and information investigation, can assist state run administrations with recognizing regions where guidelines can be gotten to the next level.

These apparatuses can examine enormous datasets and administrative archives to pinpoint areas of overt repetitiveness, irregularity, or failure. By bridling the force of innovation, legislatures can settle on information driven choices to improve their administrative systems.

Global participation and the harmonization of guidelines across borders are critical in an undeniably globalized world. Organizations frequently work in different nations and should explore assorted administrative conditions. Global principles and arrangements can work with the smoothing out of guidelines, lessening the consistence trouble for organizations participated in cross-line exchange.

For instance, associations like the World Exchange Association (WTO) and local exchange coalitions work to lay out normal principles and rules to work with global exchange. By embracing global guidelines, nations can work on their administrative necessities for organizations took part in product and import exercises. This decreases consistence costs and advances worldwide monetary reconciliation.

The advantages of smoothing out guidelines and administrative cycles are various and significant. By lessening the managerial weight on organizations, state run administrations can advance business and financial development. SMEs, specifically, stand to acquire as they frequently miss the mark on assets to explore complex administrative scenes. Rearranged and more proficient guidelines can prompt expanded business creation and development, bringing about work creation and improved monetary intensity.

Smoothed out guidelines additionally cultivate advancement and venture. At the point when organizations are not troubled by over the top administration, they can dispense more assets to innovative work, new item advancement, and market extension. This can prompt expanded seriousness on the worldwide stage, helping both individual organizations and the more extensive economy.

Moreover, improved on guidelines can prompt expense investment funds for organizations. Diminished regulatory and consistence costs permit organizations to apportion assets all the more effectively, bringing about expanded benefit. These expense reserve funds can be reinvested in extending activities, recruiting more workers, or working on the nature of items and administrations.

For shoppers, smoothed out guidelines can prompt better admittance to labor and products. Scaled down administrative hindrances can invigorate rivalry, prompting a more extensive scope of decisions and possibly lower costs. In addition, organizations that work with more noteworthy effectiveness and decreased consistence expenses might give a portion of these reserve funds to purchasers.

Natural advantages can likewise be acknowledged through administrative smoothing out. By lessening managerial obstacles and working on the administrative cycle, states can make it simpler for organizations to embrace harmless to the ecosystem practices and advances. For instance, smoothing out allowing processes for sustainable power ventures can speed up the progress to a greener economy. Improved on guidelines can likewise urge organizations to take on manageable practices that lessen asset utilization and waste.

Moreover, a smoothed out administrative climate can improve government productivity. By killing pointless administrative methodology and diminishing administrative intricacy, government organizations can dispense their assets all the more successfully. This can prompt superior public administrations, decreased stand by times, and a more responsive government, which benefits residents and organizations the same.

Chapter 7

Financial Support and Resources

Monetary help and assets are fundamental parts of financial development, business improvement, and individual thriving. Admittance to subsidizing, monetary schooling, and help with overseeing monetary assets are major to the outcome of organizations and people the same. In this article, we will investigate the significance of monetary help and assets, analyzing how they add to financial prosperity, business development, and monetary strength.

Monetary help and assets are vital for people to accomplish their monetary objectives, whether that includes homeownership, advanced education, retirement reserve funds, or beginning a private company. An absence of admittance to monetary assets can ruin individual and financial turn of events, setting out imbalances and restricting open doors for people and networks.

One of the essential wellsprings of monetary help for people is admittance to credit. Credit permits people to make significant interests in their future, like purchasing a home, seeking after advanced education, or beginning a business. Notwithstanding, numerous people face boundaries to getting to credit because of elements like low pay, restricted record of loan repayment, or unfortunate FICO ratings.

Endeavors to grow admittance to credit and monetary assets are fundamental to engage people to accomplish their monetary objectives. Drives that advance monetary consideration, for example, microloans, credit-building programs, and mindful loaning rehearses, can assist people with getting to the credit they need to put resources into their future. These projects can be especially helpful for underserved networks and minimized populaces.

Besides, monetary schooling and education assume a basic part in assisting people with settling on informed monetary choices. Admittance to monetary assets is just significant assuming people have the information and abilities to successfully deal with their funds. Monetary education projects can furnish people with the instruments and data they need to pursue wise monetary decisions, from planning and saving to effective money management and retirement arranging.

Organizations, particularly little and medium-sized endeavors (SMEs), likewise depend on monetary help and assets to begin, develop, and flourish. Admittance to capital is a huge driver of business achievement. Business people frequently expect financing to foster items, extend activities, recruit workers, and enter new business sectors. Without sufficient monetary help, organizations might battle to accomplish their maximum capacity.

Different wellsprings of monetary help are accessible to organizations, going from conventional bank advances to funding and private backers. Taxpayer supported initiatives and drives additionally offer monetary help to energize business improvement and occupation creation. These projects might incorporate awards, advance certifications, and expense motivators to help business development and advancement.

Admittance to monetary assets is particularly significant for new companies and imaginative organizations. These endeavors frequently face higher dangers and need monetary help to transform their thoughts into the real world. New companies can profit from admittance to beginning phase subsidizing, business hatcheries, and mentorship projects to assist them with exploring the difficulties of business.

Monetary assets are not restricted to subsidizing alone. Admittance to monetary administrations, for example, installment handling, finance the executives, and protection, is vital for organizations to work effectively and safeguard their inclinations. Smoothing out these monetary administrations through computerized devices and stages can assist organizations with setting aside time and cash, permitting them to zero in on their center tasks and development.

Also, organizations can profit from monetary schooling and assets that improve their monetary administration capacities. Understanding fiscal summaries, overseeing income, and upgrading capital allotment are fundamental abilities for entrepreneurs and chiefs. Monetary instruction projects and assets custom fitted to the requirements of organizations can engage them to go with informed choices that drive development and benefit.

The monetary help and assets accessible to organizations are fundamental for their prosperity as well as assume an essential part in work creation and financial turn of events. SMEs are significant supporters of occupation development in numerous economies, and they are in many cases the motors of advancement and neighborhood monetary turn of events.

Thusly, supporting these organizations with admittance to monetary assets is basic to encouraging financial development and flourishing.

Notwithstanding individual and business monetary help, monetary assets are necessary to local area advancement. Networks flourish when they approach monetary administrations, support for neighborhood organizations, and assets to put resources into framework, schooling, and medical services. These assets add to a more excellent of life, expanded monetary open door, and worked on generally speaking prosperity.

Monetary incorporation endeavors that give networks admittance to banking administrations and reasonable credit are urgent for financial turn of events. Banking administrations permit people to save, access credit, and make secure monetary exchanges, which can assist with lifting them out of destitution and give a way to financial versatility. In addition, reasonable credit can engage business people to begin or grow organizations, making position and supporting neighborhood economies.

Monetary help for local area advancement can likewise come as government awards and appropriations for foundation projects, lodging drives, and instructive projects. These speculations work on the personal satisfaction for inhabitants, draw in new organizations and occupants to the area, and animate financial development.

Monetary assets are basic to building versatile networks that can endure financial shocks and debacles. Admittance to protection and hazard the executives techniques can assist people and networks with safeguarding their resources and jobs despite unforeseen difficulties. Local area level monetary assets can be utilized to foster fiasco readiness and reaction plans, guaranteeing that occupants and organizations can recuperate from interruptions all the more successfully.

Besides, monetary assets can uphold interests in schooling and labor force advancement. Instructive projects that give grants, awards, and professional preparation can assist people with securing the abilities expected to seek after significant and well-paying vocations. A knowledgeable and talented labor force is fundamental for neighborhood organizations to flourish and contend in a worldwide economy.

7.1 Access to Capital: Loans, Grants, and Investments

Admittance to capital is a basic part of monetary development, business improvement, and individual monetary prosperity. Whether it's for beginning a business, chasing after advanced education, purchasing a home, or putting resources into creative tasks, people and organizations frequently require monetary assets to accomplish their objectives. In this article, we will dig into the significance of admittance to capital, investigating different wellsprings of capital, like advances, awards, and ventures, and how they add to financial thriving and individual achievement.

Admittance to capital is indispensable for people who try to accomplish their monetary objectives and work on their personal satisfaction. These objectives can incorporate homeownership, advanced education, retirement arranging, or in any event, beginning a private company. Capital gives the necessary resources to make significant interests in one's future, and an absence of admittance to monetary assets can prompt neglected desires, disparities, and restricted open doors for individual and local area improvement.

One of the essential wellsprings of capital for people is credit, which permits them to make huge interests in their future. Credit can be instrumental in working with significant life altering situations, like buying a home, chasing after an advanced degree, or beginning a business. In any case, numerous people face obstructions to getting to credit because of elements like low pay, restricted financial record, or unfortunate FICO assessments.

Endeavors to extend admittance to credit and monetary assets are fundamental to engage people to accomplish their monetary objectives. Drives that advance monetary consideration, for example, microloans, credit-building programs, and dependable loaning rehearses, can assist people with getting to the credit they need to put resources into their future. These projects can be especially helpful for underserved networks and minimized populaces.

Besides, monetary training and proficiency assume a basic part in assisting people with pursuing informed monetary choices. Admittance to monetary assets is just significant on the off chance that people have the information and abilities to actually deal with their funds. Monetary education projects can furnish people with the apparatuses and data they need to pursue wise monetary decisions, from planning and saving to effective money management and retirement arranging.

Admittance to capital isn't restricted to people; organizations, particularly little and medium-sized undertakings (SMEs), additionally depend on monetary help and assets to begin, develop, and flourish. Admittance to capital is a critical driver of business achievement. Business visionaries frequently expect financing to foster items, extend activities, recruit representatives, and enter new business sectors. Without sufficient admittance to monetary assets, organizations might battle to accomplish their maximum capacity.

Different wellsprings of capital are accessible to organizations, going from customary bank credits to funding and private backers. Taxpayer supported initiatives and drives likewise offer monetary help to energize business improvement and occupation creation. These projects might incorporate awards, credit certifications, and duty motivators to help business development and advancement.

Admittance to capital is particularly significant for new companies and creative organizations. These undertakings frequently face higher dangers and need monetary help to transform their thoughts into the real world.

New companies can profit from admittance to beginning phase financing, business hatcheries, and mentorship projects to assist them with exploring the difficulties of business.

Monetary assets are essential to business achievement, and admittance to capital can have a massive effect in whether a business can flourish or just make due. Satisfactory capital permits organizations to put resources into innovative work, extend product offerings, arrive at new business sectors, and recruit the ability important to drive development. With admittance to capital, organizations can take advantage of chances, answer market changes, and stay cutthroat.

In addition, monetary assets are not restricted to subsidizing alone. Admittance to monetary administrations, for example, installment handling, finance the board, and protection, is significant for organizations to work effectively and safeguard their inclinations. Smoothing out these monetary administrations through advanced apparatuses and stages can assist organizations with setting aside time and cash, permitting them to zero in on their center tasks and development.

What's more, organizations can profit from monetary training and assets that improve their monetary administration abilities. Understanding budget reports, overseeing income, and improving capital assignment are fundamental abilities for entrepreneurs and supervisors. Monetary training projects and assets customized to the necessities of organizations can enable them to settle on informed choices that drive development and productivity.

The monetary help and assets accessible to organizations are fundamental for their prosperity as well as assume a crucial part in work creation and financial turn of events. SMEs are significant supporters of occupation development in numerous economies, and they are much of the time the motors of advancement and neighborhood monetary turn of events. Hence, supporting these organizations with admittance to monetary assets is basic to cultivating financial development and success.

Extending admittance to capital is especially significant with regards to encouraging advancement and seriousness. Admittance to capital can enable organizations to put resources into innovative work, embrace new advances, and make imaginative items and administrations. This development can drive financial development, upgrade efficiency, and position organizations for progress in a quickly advancing worldwide economy.

Moreover, admittance to capital is fundamental for cultivating business venture, particularly among underserved and underrepresented populaces. Business is a strong motor for work creation, monetary turn of events, and social versatility. By giving admittance to cash-flow to business visionaries, networks can support business creation, work development, and a more evenhanded conveyance of monetary open door.

The monetary help and assets accessible to organizations are not restricted to subsidizing alone. Admittance to monetary administrations, for example, installment handling, finance the executives, and protection, is vital for organizations to work productively and safeguard their inclinations. Smoothing out these monetary administrations through advanced instruments and stages can assist organizations with setting aside time and cash, permitting them to zero in on their center activities and development.

Monetary assets are essential to building strong networks that can endure financial shocks and fiascos. Admittance to protection and hazard the executives methodologies can assist people and networks with safeguarding their resources and jobs despite surprising difficulties. Local area level monetary assets can be utilized to foster catastrophe readiness and reaction plans, guaranteeing that inhabitants and organizations can recuperate from disturbances all the more actually.

Besides, monetary assets can uphold interests in training and labor force improvement. Instructive projects that give grants, awards, and professional preparation can assist people with securing the abilities expected to seek after significant and well-paying vocations. A knowledgeable and talented labor force is fundamental for nearby organizations to flourish and contend in a worldwide economy.

Admittance to capital isn't just significant for people and organizations yet in addition assumes a critical part in local area improvement. Networks flourish when they approach monetary administrations, support for neighborhood organizations, and assets to put resources into framework, instruction, medical care, and other fundamental administrations. These assets add to a more excellent of life, expanded monetary open door, and worked on by and large prosperity.

Monetary consideration endeavors that furnish networks with admittance to banking administrations and reasonable credit are critical for financial turn of events. Banking administrations permit people to save, access credit, and make secure monetary exchanges, which can assist with lifting them out of destitution and give a way to financial portability. Besides, reasonable credit can engage business people to begin or grow organizations, making position and supporting neighborhood economies.

Monetary help for local area advancement can likewise come as government awards and sponsorships for foundation projects, lodging drives, and instructive projects. These ventures work on the personal satisfaction for inhabitants, draw in new organizations and occupants to the area, and animate financial development.

7.2 Financial Education for Small Business Owners

Monetary training for entrepreneurs is a critical component in their way to progress. Private companies assume a huge part in driving financial development, making position, and cultivating advancement. Notwithstanding, numerous entrepreneurs face monetary difficulties that can prevent their tasks and development. By furnishing them with monetary schooling and assets, entrepreneurs can settle on informed choices, deal with their funds successfully, and flourish in a serious business climate.

Monetary instruction for entrepreneurs envelops a scope of themes and abilities that are fundamental for their prosperity. These themes can incorporate monetary administration, planning, income the executives, bookkeeping, tax assessment, funding choices, and hazard the board. How about we investigate why monetary schooling is significant for entrepreneurs and how it can prompt better navigation, development, and monetary strength.

One of the essential justifications for why monetary training is fundamental for entrepreneurs is that it engages them to pursue informed choices. Monetary education outfits entrepreneurs with the information and abilities to grasp their budget reports, decipher key monetary proportions, and evaluate the monetary strength of their organizations. This understanding empowers them to distinguish areas of progress and go with informed choices to address monetary difficulties.

Additionally, monetary training helps entrepreneurs in creating powerful planning and monetary administration abilities. Planning is a basic part of business tasks, permitting entrepreneurs to designate assets proficiently and plan for both present moment and long haul monetary requirements. By dominating planning methods, entrepreneurs can abstain from overspending, expand productivity, and guarantee they have adequate assets to cover their monetary commitments.

Compelling income the board is one more basic part of monetary training for entrepreneurs. Income issues, like late installments from clients or surprising costs, can upset business activities and lead to monetary challenges. Monetary training furnishes entrepreneurs with the devices to screen and deal with their income successfully, guaranteeing that they have sufficient liquidity to meet their monetary responsibilities and put resources into business development.

Understanding bookkeeping standards and practices is additionally essential for entrepreneurs. Monetary instruction can assist entrepreneurs with appreciating fiscal reports, for example, pay articulations, asset reports, and income proclamations. This information empowers them to follow their business' monetary exhibition, settle on information driven choices, and discuss successfully with bookkeepers and monetary experts.

Tax collection is another region where monetary schooling is priceless. Entrepreneurs need to explore a perplexing trap of expense guidelines, derivations, and detailing necessities. Monetary instruction furnishes them with the information to upgrade their assessment techniques, diminish their expense responsibility, and guarantee consistence with charge regulations. Proficient duty the executives can bring about critical investment funds and worked on monetary solidness.

Admittance to different funding choices is a vital thought for entrepreneurs. Monetary training can assist them with grasping the advantages and disadvantages of various funding strategies, like credits, credit extensions, funding, and heavenly messenger ventures. Outfitted with this information, entrepreneurs can pick the supporting choice that best suits their necessities, whether it's to finance business extension, cover working capital prerequisites, or send off another item or administration.

Besides, monetary instruction gives entrepreneurs a complete comprehension of the dangers related with their business tasks. Risk the executives is a fundamental part of monetary independent direction, as organizations face different dangers, including market changes, contest, lawful and administrative issues, and financial slumps. Entrepreneurs should be furnished with the abilities to recognize, evaluate, and relieve these dangers really.

Monetary instruction can likewise add to worked on private monetary prosperity for entrepreneurs. Frequently, business and individual budgets are firmly entwined, particularly in the beginning phases of a business. Understanding how to oversee individual budgets can assist entrepreneurs with keeping up with monetary steadiness, diminish pressure, and work on their general personal satisfaction.

Admittance to monetary training and assets can fundamentally add to the development and progress of private companies. Here are a few vital manners by which monetary schooling can help entrepreneurs and their endeavors:

Further developed Navigation: Monetary schooling outfits entrepreneurs with the information and abilities to come to informed conclusions about their organizations. This incorporates planning, monetary administration, and venture choices. Informed navigation can prompt better asset designation, cost decrease, and income development.

Upgraded Monetary Security: Independent companies frequently face monetary difficulties and changes. Monetary schooling assists entrepreneurs with creating systems to keep up with monetary dependability, oversee income successfully, and explore financial vulnerabilities.

Admittance to Supporting: Monetary training gives experiences into different funding choices, empowering entrepreneurs to get to capital when required. This can be vital for business development, interest in new items or administrations, and overseeing working capital.

Proficient Duty The executives: Understanding expense guidelines and systems can assist entrepreneurs with limiting their assessment responsibility and guarantee consistence with charge regulations. Effective expense the executives can bring about huge expense reserve funds and further developed productivity.

Better Gamble The board: Monetary training furnishes entrepreneurs with risk the executives abilities, permitting them to distinguish, survey, and moderate likely dangers. This can safeguard the business from monetary misfortunes and interruptions.

Long haul Arranging: Entrepreneurs frequently center around everyday tasks, except monetary schooling urges them to take part in long haul arranging. This incorporates retirement arranging, progression arranging, and leave methodologies, guaranteeing the business' supportability and the proprietor's monetary security.

Individual Monetary Prosperity: Further developed individual monetary administration abilities can prompt more noteworthy monetary prosperity for entrepreneurs. This incorporates better control of individual budgets, lessening monetary pressure, and upgrading generally speaking personal satisfaction.

Business Development and Development: With a strong comprehension of monetary standards, entrepreneurs are better situated to put resources into advancement, extend their item or administration contributions, and investigate new business sectors. This can drive business development and seriousness.

Notwithstanding the advantages for individual entrepreneurs, monetary instruction can add to the more extensive financial scene. Private companies are critical supporters of occupation creation and monetary development, making their prosperity fundamental for generally speaking financial prosperity. At the point when private ventures are monetarily steady and outfitted with sound monetary administration abilities, they are bound to flourish and drive financial advancement in their networks.

The job of government, instructive foundations, and industry relationship in giving monetary schooling to entrepreneurs is instrumental. These substances can offer preparation projects, studios, and assets customized to the particular necessities of private ventures. Monetary instruction drives ought to cover a scope of points, including monetary administration, planning, income the executives, bookkeeping, tax collection, supporting choices, and hazard the board.

Government offices can cooperate with instructive establishments and industry relationship to create and carry out monetary schooling programs for entrepreneurs. These projects can be offered on the web, face to face, or through a blend of both, making them open to a different scope of entrepreneurs. It's critical that these projects are intended to be easy to use, reasonable, and zeroed in on true situations.

Monetary schooling for entrepreneurs ought to be a continuous exertion. The business scene is continually developing, and monetary prescribed procedures might change after some time. Accordingly, nonstop learning and admittance to cutting-edge assets are vital for keep entrepreneurs educated and furnished with the abilities they need to succeed.

All in all, monetary training for entrepreneurs is a basic part of their prosperity. Independent ventures are critical drivers of monetary development and occupation creation, and furnishing entrepreneurs with monetary information and abilities can prompt better direction, monetary strength, and development. Admittance to monetary training and assets is fundamental for enabling entrepreneurs.

7.3 The Role of Governments and Financial Institutions

The job of state run administrations and monetary establishments is critical in guaranteeing the strength and development of economies, as well as in advancing monetary consideration, and defending the interests of people and organizations. Legislatures and monetary organizations work inseparably to establish an administrative climate that encourages financial development, gives admittance to monetary administrations, and guarantees the respectability and solidness of the monetary framework. In this article, we will dive into the basic jobs played by states and monetary establishments and how their joint effort is principal to a sound and strong monetary biological system.

States play a multi-layered part in managing and directing monetary frameworks. These jobs are not just significant in keeping up with the strength of the monetary area yet in addition in defending the interests of purchasers and encouraging financial development. Coming up next are a portion of the key jobs that legislatures play in monetary business sectors:

Guideline and Oversight: Legislatures lay out and uphold administrative systems that oversee monetary establishments, including banks, credit associations, and trading companies. Administrative bodies are answerable for guaranteeing that these organizations work with trustworthiness and in consistence with laid out rules. This guideline is fundamental in forestalling misrepresentation, negligence, and foundational takes a chance with that can weaken monetary business sectors.

Money related Strategy: National banks, frequently worked or impacted by the public authority, assume a basic part in setting and carrying out financial approach. They control the cash supply, set loan costs, and oversee expansion to guarantee value security and backing financial development.

Financial Arrangement: State run administrations use monetary strategy to oversee public funds, including tax collection and government spending. Legitimate financial administration can significantly affect monetary security and development. State run administrations change monetary strategy in light of financial circumstances, planning to animate financial movement during slumps and control extreme development during financial rises.

Shopper Security: State run administrations work to safeguard the interests of purchasers by laying out regulations and guidelines connected with monetary items and administrations. These guidelines guarantee straightforwardness, fair loaning rehearses, and the defending of shopper resources. Buyer assurance organizations and ombudsman workplaces may likewise be laid out to deal with objections and debates.

Monetary Consideration: Advancing monetary incorporation is a critical job for states. Admittance to banking administrations, credit, and monetary schooling is fundamental for people and organizations to partake in the formal monetary framework. State run administrations frequently execute projects to improve monetary education and grow admittance to monetary administrations, especially for underserved and underestimated populaces.

Emergency The executives: in the midst of monetary emergencies, states assume a crucial part in balancing out the monetary framework. They might give crisis monetary help to foundations, present liquidity support projects, or carry out monetary upgrade measures to relieve the effect of monetary slumps.

Market Oversight: Government offices screen monetary business sectors to guarantee fair and proficient tasks. They additionally manage protections and wares trades to forestall market control, insider exchanging, and other unlawful exercises that can hurt financial backers and market respectability.

Monetary organizations, then again, incorporate banks, credit associations, insurance agency, venture companies, and different substances that offer monetary types of assistance to people and organizations. These organizations act as delegates that work with the progression of capital and hazard the executives in the economy. Their jobs incorporate different capabilities, including:

Intermediation: Banks and monetary establishments work with the progression of assets among savers and borrowers. They gather stores from people and substances and give advances and credit to borrowers, including organizations and people looking for contracts, individual credits, and that's only the tip of the iceberg.

Risk The board: Insurance agency assume a crucial part in risk the executives. They give inclusion against different dangers, for example, property harm, medical problems, and mishaps. By offering protection items, they assist people and organizations with safeguarding their resources and monetary prosperity.

Speculation Administrations: Trading companies and resource the board organizations help people and associations in dealing with their ventures. They offer different monetary items, including shared reserves, trade exchanged reserves (ETFs), and resource the board administrations, permitting clients to expand and upgrade their portfolios.

Installment and Settlement Administrations: Monetary organizations give installment and repayment administrations, empowering people and organizations to proficiently go through with exchanges. These administrations incorporate installment handling, wire moves, and other installment techniques that support the worldwide monetary framework.

Monetary Exhortation and Arranging: Numerous monetary establishments offer monetary counsel and arranging administrations to assist people and organizations with coming to informed conclusions about their monetary future. This incorporates retirement arranging, speculation procedures, and hazard the executives.

Capital Raising: Venture banks and guarantors help organizations in raising capital through starting public contributions (Initial public offerings) and the issuance of protections. This cycle is significant for organizations hoping to extend, finance new activities, or work with consolidations and acquisitions.

The coordinated effort among states and monetary establishments is imperative for keeping up with monetary steadiness and guaranteeing the legitimate working of the monetary framework. Here are a few key regions where their coordinated effort is basic:

Administrative Consistence: Monetary foundations should comply to a perplexing trap of guidelines laid out by legislatures. Administrative consistence is fundamental to guarantee that organizations work with trustworthiness, safeguard customers, and alleviate dangers to the monetary framework. Cooperation among controllers and monetary organizations is important with decipher, carry out, and comply to these guidelines.

Emergency The executives: in the midst of monetary emergencies, legislatures frequently work intimately with monetary organizations to resolve foundational issues. This might include giving crisis liquidity support, executing upgrade measures, and cooperating to balance out the monetary framework. Coordinated effort is essential in exploring and relieving the effects of emergencies.

Monetary Consideration: Legislatures and monetary organizations frequently team up to extend monetary incorporation. Taxpayer supported initiatives and drives might work in association with monetary foundations to reach underserved networks and give admittance to banking administrations, credit, and monetary training.

Customer Security: Cooperation among legislatures and monetary establishments is fundamental to guarantee shoppers are safeguarded. State run administrations lay out regulations and guidelines with defend buyer interests, and monetary organizations should comply to these guidelines while likewise embracing inner measures to safeguard shoppers.

Market Oversight: Government organizations regulate monetary business sectors to guarantee fair and straightforward tasks. Monetary organizations assume a pivotal part in following business sector guidelines and helping out controllers to keep up with market trustworthiness.

Money related Approach Execution: National banks, as a feature of the public authority, frequently team up with monetary organizations to carry out financial strategy. Monetary foundations are basic in sending financial approach choices by changing loan costs and dealing with the cash supply.

Chapter 8

Nurturing Entrepreneurship

Sustaining business is a mind boggling and complex undertaking that assumes a urgent part in the development and improvement of economies around the world. Business venture is the main thrust behind advancement, work creation, and financial advancement. It cultivates a culture of independence and enables people to seek after their fantasies and thoughts. In this paper, we will investigate the significance of supporting business venture, the different variables that add to its turn of events, and the job of training, government strategies, and the business climate in cultivating a dynamic pioneering biological system.

Business is much of the time portrayed as the method involved with recognizing open doors, making worth, and facing challenges to take advantage of those valuable open doors. It includes the commencement and the board of another endeavor or the rebuilding of a current association to gain by amazing open doors. Business people are people who have the vision, assurance, and drive to transform their thoughts into the real world, and in doing as such, they contribute altogether to monetary development and occupation creation.

One of the essential justifications for why sustaining business venture is fundamental is its part in driving development. Business venture urges people to think inventively, distinguish neglected needs, and foster imaginative arrangements. It's a strong power for mechanical headway and the improvement of new items and administrations. Developments driven by pioneering adventures frequently significantly affect society, prompting worked on personal satisfaction, expanded productivity, and improved seriousness in the worldwide market.

Besides, business venture is a basic driver of occupation creation. New companies and independent ventures are the foundation of numerous economies, and they are liable for a significant piece of new position valuable open doors. As indicated by information from the U.S.

Private venture Organization, independent ventures represented 44% of private-area work in the US in 2020. Business visionaries make occupations for themselves as well as recruit and train workers, adding to generally speaking business development.

Notwithstanding financial development and occupation creation, supporting business likewise advances monetary versatility. Enterprising endeavors frequently display flexibility and spryness, which permits them to answer changing economic situations. They are bound to develop and turn their plans of action in light of disturbances, like monetary slumps or unanticipated difficulties. A different and dynamic pioneering environment can assist economies with enduring financial tempests all the more successfully.

Training assumes a urgent part in sustaining business venture. It furnishes people with the information and abilities expected to recognize open doors, foster business ideas, and deal with the intricacies of maintaining a business. Business venture instruction can happen at different levels, from essential and auxiliary schools to colleges and particular preparation programs.

At the essential and optional school levels, understudies can profit from fundamental openness to business ideas. Programs like Junior Accomplishment and other extracurricular exercises show youngsters business venture, monetary education, and the worth of advancement. These early encounters can sow the seeds of business in the personalities of youthful people and rouse them to seek after their own endeavors from here on out.

Advanced education organizations, for example, colleges and universities, assume a urgent part in giving more top to bottom business schooling. Numerous colleges offer devoted business programs, where understudies can find out about business arranging, promoting, money, and the executives. These projects frequently give active encounters, including valuable chances to foster strategies, partake in business rivalries, and team up with guides and industry specialists.

Notwithstanding formal training, casual and experiential advancing likewise add to business improvement. Temporary jobs, apprenticeships, and mentorship projects can open people to the functional parts of beginning and maintaining a business. Gaining from genuine encounters and cooperating with effective business people can be important in supporting enterprising abilities and attitude.

Government strategies and guidelines assume a basic part in establishing a climate helpful for business venture. A strong administrative system can work with the foundation and development of new organizations while limiting obstructions and dangers. A few critical parts of government strategy that influence business venture incorporate tax collection, licensed innovation insurance, admittance to capital, and administrative consistence.

Charge strategies can essentially affect business venture. Positive duty motivations, for example, tax reductions for innovative work or expense allowances for private ventures, can diminish the monetary weight on business people and boost interest in development and occupation creation. Then again, complicated and difficult assessment guidelines can deflect expected business visionaries from beginning organizations.

Licensed innovation assurance is fundamental for encouraging advancement and business venture. Business people need confirmation that their licensed innovation, like licenses, brand names, and copyrights, will be shielded. Solid legitimate assurances urge business people to put resources into innovative work and put up new items and administrations for sale to the public.

Admittance to capital is a basic figure business. Fire up adventures frequently require monetary assets to subsidize research, improvement, promoting, and starting activities. Government-upheld programs, for example, private company credits and awards, can give truly necessary cash-flow to business visionaries who could somehow battle to get funding from conventional sources like banks.

Administrative consistence can be a critical boundary for business people. Unnecessary organization and formality can make it trying to begin and maintain a business. Smoothing out and working on administrative cycles, especially for private companies, can urge more individuals to set out on pioneering ventures.

Government strategies can likewise assume a part in advancing business venture through open obtainment. State run administrations can uphold neighborhood business people by giving them special treatment while granting contracts for labor and products. This can give a significant market to new pursuits and assist them with setting up a good foundation for themselves and develop.

The business climate is one more basic consider supporting business. A positive business climate envelops different components, including framework, admittance to business sectors, and the accessibility of gifted work.

Foundation, like transportation, correspondence, and utilities, is fundamental for the smooth activity of organizations. Solid foundation lessens working expenses and further develops openness, making it more straightforward for business people to arrive at clients and providers.

Admittance to business sectors is essential for business visionaries hoping to sell their items or administrations. Both nearby and global business sectors should be available to organizations, all things considered. Economic accords and drives that lessen exchange hindrances can open up new open doors for business visionaries to grow their scope.

The accessibility of gifted work is another significant thought. Business people need admittance to a labor force with the essential abilities and mastery to help their organizations. A knowledgeable and prepared labor force can add to the achievement and development of enterprising endeavors.

Moreover, the accessibility of encouraging groups of people and business hatcheries can be instrumental in sustaining business venture. These associations give assets, mentorship, and systems administration valuable open doors to business people, assisting them with exploring the difficulties of beginning and growing a business.

Business isn't restricted to conventional for-benefit organizations. Social business venture is an inexorably significant and effective part of business venture that spotlights on tending to social and natural difficulties. Social business people foster inventive answers for cultural issues and endeavor to make positive social and natural results close by monetary manageability.

Social business venture frequently includes a profound obligation to having a constructive outcome on the planet. It can envelop a large number of drives, from clean energy projects and feasible horticulture to medical services developments and instructive projects for underserved networks. Sustaining social business requires a biological system that upholds these drives and values their main goal driven approach.

Notwithstanding the different elements talked about over, the social and mental parts of business are additionally urgent. The pioneering mentality is portrayed by characteristics, for example, imagination, risk-taking, strength, and an eagerness to gain from disappointment. Developing this mentality is imperative for supporting business venture.

Social variables can impact the inclination for business venture inside a general public. A culture that values business and praises its triumphs can propel people to seek after enterprising endeavors. Besides, social acknowledgment of disappointment as a learning opportunity as opposed to a shame can urge more individuals to face challenges and begin organizations.

Mental variables assume a huge part in the choice to turn into a business visionary. Individual credits like fearlessness, assurance, and a solid feeling of direction are frequently connected with effective business people. Empowering and supporting these characteristics can assist people with conquering the apprehension about disappointment and bring the jump into business.

8.1 Entrepreneurship Education and Training

Business venture schooling and preparing assume a critical part in molding the eventual fate of business and monetary scenes. In a consistently impacting world driven by development, business venture isn't simply a lifelong decision; a mentality encourages imagination, development, and critical thinking. To support the up and coming age of business people and empower people to flourish in the present powerful business climate, giving them the right schooling and training is urgent.

Business venture schooling isn't restricted to beginning and maintaining a business. It includes a wide range of information and abilities that engage people to recognize potential open doors, foster imaginative arrangements, and drive change. The center components of business venture schooling and preparing include:

Thought Age and Imagination: Business venture begins with a good thought. Schooling and preparing projects ought to urge people to think inventively, distinguish neglected needs, and produce creative arrangements. Imagination is the fuel that powers business.

Opportunity Acknowledgment: The capacity to perceive potential open doors in the market is central to business venture. People need to figure out how to examine the climate, break down patterns, and spot holes or shortcomings that can be transformed into business open doors.

Business Arranging: Fostering a strong strategy is a basic move toward transforming a thought into a reasonable endeavor. Business venture schooling ought to show the standards of business arranging, including statistical surveying, monetary guaging, and methodology improvement.

Risk The executives: Business intrinsically implies risk. Schooling and preparing projects ought to help people comprehend and oversee risk really. This incorporates monetary gamble, market chance, and individual gamble.

Monetary Proficiency: A fundamental part of business venture is overseeing funds. Business visionaries need to grasp fiscal summaries, planning, and income the executives to guarantee the maintainability of their endeavors.

Advertising and Deals: Compelling showcasing and deals systems are imperative for the progress of any business. Business venture schooling ought to cover points like marking, client procurement, and deals strategies.

Systems administration and Relationship Building: Building an organization of associations is significant for business people. Schooling and preparing ought to show people how to lay out and keep up with significant associations with guides, clients, providers, and friends.

Development and Innovation: In the present quick moving world, innovation and advancement are key to business venture. Instruction and preparing ought to give experiences into arising advances, computerized showcasing, and problematic plans of action.

Morals and Social Obligation: A solid moral establishment is fundamental for business visionaries. Training ought to stress the significance of moral strategic approaches and social obligation.

Disappointment and Flexibility: Business frequently includes mishaps and disappointments. Preparing ought to furnish people with the flexibility and critical thinking abilities important to return quickly from difficulties.

Business venture schooling and preparing can take different structures, contingent upon the main interest group and the ideal results. Here are a portion of the vital ways to deal with conveying business training:

1. **Formal Schooling:** Numerous colleges and universities offer proper degree programs in business. These projects frequently incorporate a blend of home-room guidance, contextual investigations, and true ventures. Understudies can

procure degrees like an Unhitched male's in Business venture or an Expert's Good to go Organization (MBA) with an emphasis on business.

2. **Proceeding with Training:** Business courses and studios are likewise accessible for people who need to become familiar with business venture without signing up for a proper degree program. These can be presented by instructive foundations, industry associations, and online stages.

3. **Web based Learning:** The web has made business venture training open to a worldwide crowd. Different web-based stages offer courses and assets on business, covering a great many points. These stages frequently give adaptability, permitting students to advance at their own speed.

4. **Hatcheries and Gas pedals:** Business venture centered programs like hatcheries and gas pedals give a steady climate to beginning phase business visionaries. They offer mentorship, admittance to assets, and some of the time even introductory financing to help new companies develop and succeed.

5. **Mentorship:** Mentorship is a significant type of business venture training. Experienced business people can give direction, share their insight, and proposition bits of knowledge striving for business people. Mentorship connections can be formal or casual.

6. **Work-Based Learning:** A few people learn business by working in new companies or private ventures. These active encounters give reasonable experiences into the difficulties and chances of business.

It's crucial for note that business venture schooling isn't just for yearning business people. The abilities and attitude developed through business venture schooling are significant in different settings, including corporate advancement, social business venture, and enterprise endeavor (pioneering exercises inside laid out associations). These abilities are adaptable and can engage people to drive positive change in their professions and networks.

The advantages of business instruction and preparing are various and wide-coming to:

1. **Cultivating Development:** Business schooling empowers inventive reasoning and critical thinking, which are fundamental for driving advancement. Developments frequently bring about better items, administrations, and cycles, helping society all in all.

2. **Work Creation:** Business schooling not just prepares people to begin their own organizations yet additionally sets them up to add to work creation in their networks. Private companies are critical wellsprings of business.

3. **Financial Development:** A flourishing enterprising environment is an impetus for monetary development. Instruction and preparing projects can assist with

developing a pool of capable business people who can send off and develop fruitful organizations, adding to financial turn of events.

4. **Flexibility:** The abilities and attitude procured through business schooling empower people to adjust to changing conditions and jump all over new chances. In a quickly developing world, flexibility is a significant resource.

5. **Critical thinking:** Business venture training imparts critical thinking abilities. Business visionaries are frequently confronted with complex difficulties, and their capacity to find savvy fixes is an important resource in any field.

6. **Strengthening:** Business venture schooling engages people to assume command over their fates. It energizes independence and drive, empowering individuals to transform their thoughts into the real world.

7. **Social Effect:** Social business venture, a part of business, centers around tending to social and natural difficulties. Schooling in this space engages people to make positive change in their networks and then some.

Nonetheless, there are difficulties and contemplations in business schooling that should be tended to:

1. **Educational program Improvement:** Creating pertinent and modern educational program is a test. The quickly changing business climate requires continuous updates to guarantee that training stays pertinent.

2. **Access and Inclusivity:** Guaranteeing admittance to business venture schooling for all people, no matter what their experience, is fundamental. Endeavors ought to be made to diminish hindrances to get to, like expense and geological limitations.

3. **Quality and Normalization:** The nature of business venture instruction projects can differ. Laying out principles and benchmarks for quality is fundamental to guarantee that students get significant instruction.

4. **Viable Experience:** While hypothesis is urgent, reasonable experience is similarly significant. Projects ought to consolidate certifiable encounters, contextual investigations, and open doors for understudies to apply what they've realized.

5. **Educator and Teacher Preparing:** Viable business venture training requires educators who grasp the topic and can move and guide understudies. Preparing for educators is significant.

6. **Assessment and Evaluation:** Estimating the viability of business venture training programs is a complicated errand. Deciding the effect of such projects on graduates and their endeavors requires progressing assessment.

7. **Empowering Chance Taking:** Business venture implies risk, and numerous people might be risk-opposed. Empowering understudies to embrace reasonable plans of action and gain from disappointment is a test.

As of late, there has been a developing acknowledgment of the significance of business venture schooling and preparing at all degrees of instruction. Legislatures, instructive foundations, and confidential associations are putting resources into programs that cultivate business venture and advancement. These drives plan to make a more enterprising society, where people are outfitted with the abilities and mentality to flourish in a quickly impacting world.

Additionally, business schooling is progressively coordinated into assorted disciplines. For instance, STEM (Science, Innovation, Designing, and Math) instruction frequently incorporates parts of business venture, as these fields are firmly connected to development and mechanical headways. Cross-disciplinary methodologies urge people to consolidate their specific information with enterprising abilities to make new items and arrangements.

8.2 Mentorship Programs and Incubators

Mentorship projects and business hatcheries assume a fundamental part in the realm of business venture. These drives give direction, backing, and assets hoping for business people, assisting them with exploring the intricacies of beginning and growing a business. While mentorship programs pair experienced business people with tenderfoots, business hatcheries offer an organized climate where new companies can thrive. Together, these roads cultivate pioneering achievement, empower advancement, and add to financial development.

Mentorship Projects:

Mentorship is an amazing asset for individual and expert development. With regards to business venture, mentorship interfaces prepared business visionaries with people who are new to the business world. This association is established on the standard of information sharing and direction. Experienced guides offer bits of knowledge, give important input, and help mentees explore the innovative scene.

One of the essential benefits of mentorship programs is the exchange of common-sense information. Coaches have regularly strolled the enterprising way, and they can share their encounters, the two triumphs and disappointments, with mentees. This firsthand information can be priceless, assisting learners with keeping away from normal traps and settle on informed choices.

Moreover, mentorship programs cultivate a feeling of local area and give admittance to significant organizations. Mentees frequently get to the tutor's business contacts, which can open ways to valuable open doors, organizations, and money sources that would have in any case been far off. The associations fashioned through mentorship can be significant in a business person's excursion.

Mentorship programs likewise offer everyday reassurance. Beginning a business can be a desolate and testing try. Having a tutor who can give support, share individual accounts of strength, and give a listening ear can assist business people with remaining persuaded and defeat the unavoidable impediments they experience.

Notwithstanding, finding the ideal tutor can be a test. The guide mentee relationship ought to be based on trust and similarity, which can find opportunity to create. It's fundamental for guides and mentees to share normal qualities, targets, and correspondence styles for the organization to find success.

Besides, successful mentorship requires devotion and time responsibility from the two players. Tutors need to apportion time to direct their mentees, and mentees should be responsive to guidance and able to execute suggested procedures. The mentorship relationship ought to be a two-way road, with the two players profiting from the experience.

Business Hatcheries:

Business hatcheries give an organized and steady climate for new companies to develop and create. These projects offer a scope of assets and administrations, including office space, admittance to capital, mentorship, and systems administration valuable open doors. Hatcheries intend to speed up the development of beginning phase organizations and increment their odds of coming out on top.

One of the essential advantages of business hatcheries is admittance to actual foundation. New companies frequently battle to get reasonable office space and admittance to vital assets. Business hatcheries give shared work areas and offices, which can essentially diminish above costs for beginning phase organizations.

Hatcheries likewise offer admittance to subsidizing and venture open doors. Numerous hatcheries have organizations with investment firms, private backers, and different wellsprings of financing. New companies inside hatchery projects might have a superior possibility protecting venture because of their relationship with a trustworthy hatchery.

Also, business hatcheries give mentorship and master direction. In-house specialists and tutors can offer important experiences on business system, advertising, finance, and other basic regions. These coaches can help new companies refine their field-tested strategies, pursue significant choices, and stay away from exorbitant mix-ups.

Organizing open doors are one more benefit of business hatcheries. Business visionaries can interface with individual new companies, guides, industry specialists, and expected clients inside the hatchery's local area. These associations can prompt organizations, joint efforts, and client acquisitions that probably won't have been imaginable in any case.

Be that as it may, joining a business hatchery isn't without challenges. Contest for section into top-level hatcheries can be furious, and not all candidates are acknowledged. Moreover, hatchery programs frequently accompany explicit assumptions and achievements that new businesses should meet. Missing the mark concerning these assumptions can bring about the end of hatchery support.

The outcome of new companies in business hatcheries can fluctuate generally. While certain organizations flourish inside the hatchery climate, others may not accomplish the ideal development or may turn out to be excessively subject to the assets gave, making it trying to change to free tasks.

All in all, mentorship projects and business hatcheries are fundamental parts of the enterprising biological system. They give hopeful business people the help, assets, and direction they need to explore the difficulties of beginning and growing a business. Whether through private mentorship or support in an organized hatchery program, business visionaries get to information, organizations, and framework that can fundamentally build their odds of coming out on top.

The decision among mentorship and business brooding frequently relies upon a business visionary's particular necessities and objectives. A few business visionaries might benefit most from the customized direction and consistent encouragement of a tutor, while others might require the extensive assets and framework of a hatchery. At times, a mix of the two methodologies might be the best procedure.

The progress of mentorship projects and business hatcheries eventually depends on the devotion, responsibility, and strength of the business visionaries included. These projects give an important structure, however it is the vision, assurance, and development of the business people themselves that drive achievement and add to the proceeded with development of the innovative scene.

8.3 Cultivating a Culture of Innovation and Creativity

Developing a culture of development and imagination is fundamental for associations looking to flourish in the present quickly advancing and cutthroat scene. It isn't restricted to innovation organizations or new businesses; rather, development and imagination are essentials for outcome in virtually every area. A culture that energizes and esteems development cultivates seriousness as well as drives development, impels variation to change, and opens new open doors.

Development and innovativeness are frequently utilized reciprocally, however they are unmistakable yet firmly associated ideas. Advancement alludes to the most common way of presenting groundbreaking thoughts, items, administrations, or practices, while imagination is the capacity to create clever thoughts, arrangements, or articulations. A culture that advances both development and imagination can assist associations with tending to difficulties, quickly jump all over chances, and separate themselves on the lookout.

1. **Initiative and Vision:**

    Developing a culture of advancement and imagination begins at the top. Pioneers set the vibe and bearing for the whole association. It is fundamental for pioneers to underwrite as well as champion development as a basic belief. They should explain a convincing vision that moves representatives to contribute their innovative thoughts and proceed with reasonable courses of action.

    Pioneers can accomplish this by encouraging a culture of mental security, where workers feel open to communicating their thoughts and testing without the anxiety toward analysis or response. Such a climate urges representatives to consider some fresh possibilities, share their experiences, and work cooperatively towards shared objectives.

2. **Open Correspondence:**

Compelling correspondence is essential to development and innovativeness. Associations should lay out open channels for thoughts to stream unreservedly from all levels and divisions. Empowering normal input, meetings to generate new ideas, and entryway strategies can assist with separating storehouses and work with thought trade.

In addition, it is fundamental for pioneers and administrators to pay attention to their representatives effectively. Representative information shouldn't just be requested yet additionally esteemed and followed up on. Along these lines, workers are bound to feel that their thoughts matter and that their innovativeness is a necessary piece of the association's development.

3. **Various Groups:**

Variety, whether concerning socioeconomics, foundations, or viewpoints, can be a strong impetus for development. A different labor force brings various thoughts, encounters, and perspectives to the table, which can prompt more imaginative critical thinking and the improvement of creative arrangements.

Associations can effectively cultivate variety and incorporation by executing enlistment and maintenance methodologies that esteem distinctions and establish a comprehensive workplace. A blend of sexual orientations, nationalities, ages, and social foundations can add to more extravagant innovativeness and development.

4. **Consolation of Hazard Taking:**

Advancement frequently implies facing challenges, as it requires wandering into the obscure and exploring different avenues regarding problematic thoughts. A culture of development embraces determined risk-taking and reevaluates disappointment as an important growth opportunity. At the point when workers won't hesitate to face challenges, they are bound to investigate inventive arrangements.

Associations can empower risk-taking by setting clear assumptions, enduring thoroughly examined disappointments, and compensating innovative undertakings. Celebrating the two victories and the fortitude to endeavor something new sends a strong message that development is profoundly respected.

5. **Time and Asset Allotment:**

Development calls for investment and assets. Associations should designate these significant resources for help imaginative and creative drives. This can include committed time for meetings to generate new ideas, interest in innovative work, and the arrangement of devices and innovation that empower advancement.

It is fundamental for associations to figure out some kind of harmony between everyday functional exercises and development endeavors. Without a promise to committing time and assets to development, it tends to be trying to develop a culture that really esteems innovativeness.

6. **Learning and Improvement:**

Associations ought to give open doors to ceaseless acquiring and expertise improvement. Representative preparation and improvement projects can upgrade workers' imaginative and critical thinking capacities. These projects can likewise acquaint workers with new advances, devices, and approaches that drive development.

Integrating advancement centered preparing into the authoritative culture guarantees that representatives are furnished with the vital abilities and information to add to imaginative and inventive undertakings. Besides, offering open doors for proficient development and ability upgrade can lift worker confidence level and commitment.

7. **Acknowledgment and Prizes:**

Perceiving and compensating development and imagination is a basic component of supporting a culture that esteems these characteristics. Prizes can come in different structures, like monetary impetuses, advancements, or public affirmation. Praising and exhibiting imaginative victories supports the significance of inventiveness as well as fills in as a motivation to other people.

Notwithstanding, associations ought to be aware of staying away from a culture of over the top contest, which can obstruct development by making an apprehension about disappointment. Finding some kind of harmony among rivalry and joint effort is urgent to keeping a solid development culture.

8. **Nonstop Input:**

Customary input circles give a way to evaluate and refine the association's development culture consistently. Studies, idea boxes, and one-on-one criticism meetings can assist with checking the degree of imagination and advancement inside the association.

This input ought to be utilized to make essential acclimations to approaches, practices, and methodologies, and to guarantee that the way of life of advancement stays lined up with the association's vision and objectives.

9. **Embracing Innovation:**

In the computerized age, innovation assumes a focal part in development. Associations need to embrace and put resources into innovation that can smooth out processes, robotize routine errands, and give information driven experiences. Additionally, innovation can work with coordinated effort and correspondence, empowering representatives to cooperate on creative tasks no matter what their actual areas.

10. **Corporate Obligation and Manageability:**

Embracing corporate obligation and manageability drives can be a strong driver of development and imagination. Associations that focus on ecological and social worries frequently track down imaginative ways of lessening waste, further develop proficiency, and foster inventive items and administrations that resound with a socially cognizant market.

11. **Statistical surveying and Client Criticism:**

    Development ought to be directed by a profound comprehension of client needs and market patterns. Associations should put resources into statistical surveying and effectively look for client criticism. This data can illuminate item advancement, administration upgrades, and cycle enhancements.

    By understanding the problem areas and wants of their main interest group, associations can fit their development endeavors to satisfy market needs successfully.

12. **Business undertaking:**

    As well as cultivating development from outside sources, associations can likewise empower enterprise endeavor. Business visionaries are representatives who take on enterprising jobs inside the association, creating and carrying out imaginative thoughts that drive development and change.

    Business undertaking programs frequently give workers independence, assets, and backing to seek after their inventive drives inside the association. These drives can prompt new items, administrations, or cycles that benefit the organization and its clients.

13. **Benchmarking and Best Practices:**

    Observing industry patterns, contenders, and best practices is fundamental. Associations can gain from others in their field and adjust effective techniques and strategies to their novel setting. Benchmarking can likewise motivate imagination by presenting representatives to creative practices outside the association.

14. **Adaptability and Flexibility:**

    Developing a culture of advancement and imagination expects associations to be adaptable and versatile. The business climate is always developing, and associations that can turn and adjust rapidly are bound to jump all over new chances and explore difficulties effectively.

15. **Assessment and Measurements:**

Assessing the adequacy of development endeavors is pivotal. Associations ought to lay out clear measurements and key execution markers (KPIs) to evaluate the effect of development on the association's main concern. This information driven approach empowers associations to tweak their advancement methodologies in view of results and adjust to changing economic situations.

Chapter 9

The Future of Small Businesses

The scene of private ventures is in a consistent condition of development, molded by a huge number of variables, including mechanical progressions, monetary moves, and changes in customer conduct. In this time of fast change, the fate of private companies is a subject of significant interest and hypothesis. To comprehend where private ventures are going, it's fundamental to inspect the vital patterns and difficulties that are probably going to affect their development and manageability.

One of the most conspicuous drivers of progress for private companies is innovation. Throughout the course of recent many years, mechanical developments have altered the manner in which organizations work, and this pattern makes it clear that things are not pulling back. Private ventures are progressively taking on advanced devices and stages to smooth out their tasks, arrive at clients, and contend in an undeniably globalized market.

The ascent of internet business, for example, has permitted independent ventures to get to an immense client base past their neighborhood or territorial business sectors. Online commercial centers and stages like Amazon, eBay, and Etsy have become life savers for the vast majority little retailers and craftsmans, giving them an instant framework to offer their items to a worldwide crowd. What's more, web-based entertainment stages have empowered independent ventures to reach and draw in with their interest groups, building brand mindfulness and client dependability.

Man-made consciousness (computer based intelligence) and mechanization are additionally changing the manner in which private companies work. From chatbots that handle client requests to computerized stock administration frameworks, man-made intelligence controlled apparatuses are assisting entrepreneurs with saving time and diminish functional expenses. Besides, AI calculations are being utilized to break down client information and give significant experiences to better navigation.

While innovation offers huge open doors for independent ventures, it additionally presents difficulties. The fast speed of mechanical change implies that entrepreneurs should persistently adjust and put resources into new apparatuses and preparing.

Network protection is one more critical worry, as private companies can be powerless against information breaks and online dangers. In this manner, guaranteeing information security and protection is a continuous need.

The worldwide economy significantly affects private ventures also. Monetary circumstances can change because of different variables, including international occasions, catastrophic events, and pandemics. The Coronavirus pandemic, for instance, devastatingly affected numerous independent companies, constraining them to close briefly or adjust to make due. Those that could turn to online activities and adjust their plans of action were bound to face the hardship.

The eventual fate of independent companies will rely upon their capacity to really answer financial changes and vulnerabilities. Building strength through monetary preparation, expansion, and dexterity will be fundamental. Independent ventures may likewise profit from government support projects and approaches that give strength during financial slumps.

Maintainability is arising as a basic component for private ventures from here on out. As buyers become more aware of ecological and social issues, organizations are supposed to line up with economical practices. This includes eco-accommodating activities as well as moral stock chains and fair work rehearses. Private companies that focus on manageability can draw in a developing section of eco-cognizant purchasers and improve their standing on the lookout.

Coordinated effort and organizations will assume a huge part coming down the line for independent companies. In an undeniably interconnected world, organizations can profit from working together with different associations, whether through joint endeavors, co-advertising endeavors, or shared assets. Associations can give admittance to new business sectors, innovations, and aptitude that would be trying to freely secure.

Administrative conditions will likewise shape the eventual fate of private companies. Legislatures assume a huge part in setting the principles and norms that organizations should follow. Private companies need to remain informed about administrative changes and guarantee consistence to keep away from lawful issues and fines. The administrative scene can change essentially by area and industry, so organizations should adjust to their particular settings.

Admittance to capital has forever been a worry for private companies, and it will keep on being a test from now on. While there are different wellsprings of financing accessible, for example, bank credits, funding, and crowdfunding, getting capital remaining parts an obstacle for some business people. Later on, private companies might have to investigate elective supporting choices, including influence effective money management, distributed loaning, and microloans.

One more essential part representing things to come of independent companies is the changing idea of work. The ascent of remote and adaptable work courses of action has the two advantages and difficulties for private companies. On one hand, remote work can empower organizations to take advantage of a worldwide ability pool and diminish above costs related with actual office spaces. Then again, overseeing remote groups and keeping major areas of strength for a culture can more test.

Private companies might have to adjust their administration and correspondence procedures to lead and connect with remote groups really. They should likewise think about the ramifications of remote work on network safety, information insurance, and representative prosperity. The eventual fate of work for private companies will require a harmony among adaptability and design to cultivate efficiency and development.

The opposition scene is consistently advancing for private ventures. They rival other independent companies as well as with bigger enterprises and tech monsters. Online business stages, for example, have made it simpler for shoppers to look at items and costs, which can put independent companies in a difficult spot on the off chance that they can't offer cutthroat evaluating and remarkable client care.

To remain cutthroat, private companies should zero in on their extraordinary offers. This can include offering customized administrations, specialty items, or extraordinary client encounters. Building an unwavering client base through trust and fulfillment will be basic for long haul achievement.

Development is the backbone of private ventures, and it will keep on being a main thrust in their future. Independent companies that advance and adjust to changing client needs and market patterns are bound to flourish. Advancement doesn't necessarily need state of the art innovation; it can include process upgrades, imaginative showcasing systems, or new item contributions.

Private ventures ought to cultivate a culture of development, support representative imagination, and put resources into innovative work. They can likewise take advantage of outside wellsprings of advancement, like associations with research establishments or cooperation in startup hatcheries and gas pedals.

The fate of independent companies will likewise be impacted by segment shifts. The maturing populace in many created nations presents amazing open doors and difficulties. Organizations that take care of the necessities of seniors, like medical services, home administrations, and relaxation exercises, are probably going to see development. In any case, they should likewise think about the effect of a contracting labor force and an expected lack of gifted work.

Simultaneously, independent ventures should adjust to the inclinations and assumptions for more youthful ages, like Twenty to thirty year olds and Age Z. These gatherings have different utilization examples, values, and correspondence styles. To speak to them, organizations might have to offer more practical and socially mindful items and participate in real, reason driven showcasing.

The globalization of business sectors is another component forming the eventual fate of private companies. Propels in transportation and correspondence innovation have made it simpler for organizations to get to worldwide business sectors. While this offers new learning experiences, it additionally presents difficulties connected with social contrasts, lawful necessities, and rivalry with neighborhood organizations.

Private companies looking to grow universally should lead exhaustive statistical surveying, grasp nearby guidelines, and adjust their items or administrations to address the issues and inclinations of worldwide clients. They may likewise have to explore exchange hindrances and taxes, which can influence their expense designs and estimating procedures.

The gig economy and outsourcing are turning out to be progressively normal, and they have suggestions for private ventures. Self employed entities and consultants offer adaptable answers for organizations, permitting them to get to specific abilities without the drawn out responsibilities of conventional business. In any case, private ventures should explore legitimate and burden contemplations while drawing in consultants, and they need to guarantee that these laborers line up with their business objectives.

Private ventures can likewise profit from the gig economy by utilizing stages like Upwork or Fiverr to get to independent ability for explicit activities or assignments. These stages give a practical method for taking advantage of a worldwide ability pool for a great many administrations.

9.1 The Ongoing Transformation of Local Economies

The scene of neighborhood economies is encountering a persistent and significant change, driven by a large number of interconnected factors that are reshaping the manner in which organizations work and networks flourish. In a time set apart by globalization, mechanical progressions, and natural worries, the fate of neighborhood economies is a fascinating subject of investigation. To acquire a far reaching comprehension of where nearby economies are going, it is fundamental to dig into the critical patterns and difficulties that are forming their development.

Innovation as an Impetus for Change

One of the most noticeable drivers of progress for nearby economies is innovation. The fast speed of mechanical development has changed the manner in which organizations capability, bringing about the two valuable open doors and difficulties. Neighborhood organizations are progressively utilizing computerized devices and stages to smooth out their tasks, arrive at clients, and stay cutthroat in a time of globalization.

Online business has arisen as a groundbreaking power in nearby economies. Private companies can now get to a tremendous client base past their nearby geographic district through web-based commercial centers and stages. Stages like Amazon, Etsy, and eBay have become indispensable channels for nearby retailers and craftsmans to grandstand their items to a worldwide crowd. Moreover, virtual entertainment stages give nearby organizations chances to draw in and associate with their objective clients, building brand mindfulness and cultivating client devotion.

Man-made brainpower (computer based intelligence) and mechanization are likewise reshaping the functional scene of neighborhood organizations. Artificial intelligence controlled apparatuses, for example, chatbots for client service or robotized stock administration frameworks, have empowered neighborhood organizations to save time and decrease functional expenses. AI calculations are utilized to break down client information, giving important experiences that illuminate better independent direction.

While innovation offers enormous open doors for neighborhood economies, it additionally presents difficulties. The fast speed of mechanical change requires neighborhood organizations to consistently adjust and put resources into new devices and worker preparing. Moreover, network safety is a critical worry as nearby organizations, frequently inadequate with regards to the assets of bigger partnerships, can be defenseless against information breaks and online dangers. It is a continuous basic to Protect information security and protection.

Monetary Circumstances and Nearby Versatility

Neighborhood economies are inherently attached to the worldwide financial climate. Financial circumstances can vacillate because of different elements, including international occasions, cataclysmic events, and monetary slumps. Neighborhood organizations are defenseless against these monetary moves and should construct strength to endure testing times.

The worldwide Coronavirus pandemic fills in as an unmistakable illustration of the effect of financial circumstances on nearby economies. Numerous neighborhood organizations had to close briefly or adjust their plans of action to get by. Those that turned to online activities and changed their techniques were bound to climate the emergency. The fate of nearby economies relies upon the capacity of organizations to answer actually to monetary changes and vulnerabilities.

To construct versatility, nearby organizations can participate in powerful monetary preparation, enhancement of income streams, and nimbleness in adjusting to advertise shifts. Government support projects and arrangements can give strength during monetary slumps, helping nearby organizations in their endeavors to make due and recuperate.

Maintainability and Moral Practices

Maintainability is arising as a basic component for neighborhood economies. As ecological and social worries gain unmistakable quality, organizations are supposed to line up with manageable practices. Maintainability incorporates eco-accommodating tasks as well as moral inventory chains and fair work rehearses. Nearby organizations that focus on supportability can draw in a developing portion of eco-cognizant purchasers and upgrade their standing on the lookout.

Coordinated effort and organizations will likewise assume a critical part coming soon for neighborhood economies. In an interconnected world, organizations can profit from coordinated efforts with different associations, whether through joint endeavors, co-promoting endeavors, or shared assets. Associations can give admittance to new business sectors, advancements, and ability that would be trying to freely obtain.

Administrative conditions are essential in molding the fate of neighborhood economies. States assume a vital part in setting the principles and guidelines that nearby organizations should comply with. Nearby organizations need to remain informed about administrative changes and guarantee consistence to keep away from legitimate issues and fines. The administrative scene can shift essentially by area and industry, requiring organizations to adjust to their particular settings.

Admittance to Capital and Subsidizing

Admittance to capital has forever been a worry for neighborhood organizations, and it will keep on being a test from now on. While different wellsprings of subsidizing are accessible, for example, bank credits, investment, and crowdfunding, getting capital remaining parts an obstacle for some business visionaries. Later on, neighborhood organizations might have to investigate elective funding choices, including influence financial planning, distributed loaning, and microloans.

With regards to neighborhood economies, local area based funding models are acquiring conspicuousness. Local area banks and credit associations assume a crucial part in offering monetary help to nearby organizations. Besides, neighborhood speculation organizations and crowdfunding stages empower networks to help nearby endeavors straightforwardly. These models encourage a feeling of shared liability regarding the financial prosperity of the local area.

The Eventual fate of Work and Nearby Economies

The changing idea of work is another basic component impacting nearby economies. The ascent of remote and adaptable work plans has the two advantages and difficulties for nearby organizations.

Remote work can empower organizations to get to a worldwide ability pool and decrease above costs related with actual office spaces. Be that as it may, overseeing remote groups and keeping major areas of strength for a culture can more test.

Nearby organizations should adjust their administration and correspondence methodologies to lead and connect with remote groups really. They should likewise think about the ramifications of remote work on network safety, information assurance, and representative prosperity. The fate of work for nearby economies will require a harmony among adaptability and design to encourage efficiency and development.

Serious Scene and Specialty Specialization

Nearby organizations are persistently exploring a cutthroat scene that has developed with the coming of innovation and globalization. They rival other nearby organizations as well as fight with bigger enterprises and tech monsters. Online business stages and cost examination devices have made it more straightforward for buyers to look at items and costs, which can put nearby organizations in a difficult spot on the off chance that they can't offer cutthroat valuing and extraordinary client support.

To stay cutthroat, neighborhood organizations should zero in on their exceptional offers. This might include offering customized administrations, specialty items, or outstanding client encounters. Building an unwavering client base through trust and fulfillment will be basic for long haul achievement.

The Basic of Advancement

Development is the backbone of nearby economies, and it will keep on being a main impetus in their future. Nearby organizations that develop and adjust to changing client needs and market patterns are bound to flourish. Advancement doesn't necessarily need state of the art innovation; it can include process enhancements, imaginative advertising techniques, or new item contributions.

Cultivating a culture of development is fundamental for neighborhood organizations. Empowering worker imagination and putting resources into innovative work can drive development from the inside. Neighborhood organizations can likewise take advantage of outer wellsprings of advancement by collaborating with research foundations or partaking in startup hatcheries and gas pedals.

Segment Movements and Neighborhood Economies

Segment shifts are critical elements that shape the fate of nearby economies. The maturing populace in many created nations presents the two open doors and difficulties. Organizations that take care of the requirements of seniors, like medical services, home administrations, and recreation exercises, are probably going to see development. Be that as it may, they should likewise think about the effect of a contracting labor force and an expected lack of talented work.

Simultaneously, neighborhood organizations should adjust to the inclinations and assumptions for more youthful ages, like Recent college grads and Age Z. These gatherings have different utilization examples, values, and correspondence styles. To speak to them, nearby organizations might have to offer more feasible and socially dependable items and take part in credible, reason driven showcasing.

Globalization and Neighborhood Economies

The globalization of business sectors is another element molding the fate of nearby economies. Propels in transportation and correspondence innovation have made it more straightforward for organizations to get to global business sectors. While this offers new learning experiences, it likewise presents difficulties connected with social contrasts, legitimate prerequisites, and rivalry with neighborhood organizations.

Neighborhood organizations looking to extend all around the world should direct careful statistical surveying, figure out nearby guidelines, and adjust their items or administrations to address the issues and inclinations of global clients. They may likewise have to explore exchange obstructions and duties, which can influence their expense designs and valuing methodologies.

9.2 Innovations and Technological Advancements

In the present high speed world, development and mechanical progressions are driving change across different enterprises and areas. The tireless walk of innovation is having an impact on the manner in which we live, work, and connect with the world. From computerized reasoning and computerization to biotechnology and clean energy arrangements, the effect of development is significant and extensive. This article investigates the developing scene of advancements and mechanical progressions and their suggestions for society, business, and the worldwide economy.

The Speed increase of Mechanical Advancement

Mechanical development has forever been a main impetus behind human advancement, yet in late many years, it has advanced at an extraordinary speed. This speed increase is because of a few interconnected factors, including expanded computational power, the multiplication of information, and the democratization of innovation. Basically, we are amidst a mechanical unrest that is reshaping ventures and social orders in significant ways.

Man-made brainpower and AI

Man-made consciousness (computer based intelligence) and AI are at the bleeding edge of mechanical progressions. These innovations are changing the scene of ventures going from medical services to fund. Computer based intelligence calculations can examine tremendous measures of information and concentrate significant bits of knowledge, going with them crucial for information driven choice making.

Artificial intelligence driven applications, for example, normal language handling and PC vision, are being utilized to robotize assignments, from client care chatbots to independent vehicles. This isn't simply a mechanical leap forward; it addresses a central change by they way we approach critical thinking and independent direction.

The ramifications of man-made intelligence and AI are significant. While they offer colossal proficiency gains and the possibility to tackle complex issues, they additionally bring up moral and cultural issues. Worries about work dislodging, information protection, and algorithmic inclination are at the front of conversations encompassing man-made intelligence. Finding some kind of harmony between tackling the advantages of artificial intelligence and tending to its difficulties is a continuous undertaking for society.

Robotization and Advanced mechanics

Robotization and advanced mechanics are changing ventures that were once vigorously dependent on human work. Assembling, operations, and even client care are seeing the mix of advanced mechanics and computerization innovations. These advancements can possibly increment proficiency, decrease functional expenses, and work on the nature of work in dangerous or dreary conditions.

Nonetheless, the rising mechanization of occupations likewise raises worries about work uprooting and the requirement for upskilling and reskilling the labor force. The eventual fate of work might include a cooperative energy among people and machines, where computerization handles dull errands, permitting people to zero in on more elevated level, imaginative, and critical thinking exercises.

Biotechnology and Medical services Advancements

Biotechnology has opened additional opportunities in medical services. Advancements in genomics, customized medication, and medication improvement are working on the comprehension and treatment of illnesses. Hereditary altering advances like CRISPR-Cas9 hold the possibility to change medical services by tending to hereditary issues at their underlying foundations.

Telemedicine and advanced wellbeing stages are upgrading admittance to medical care administrations, particularly in remote or underserved regions. Wearable gadgets and wellbeing applications are permitting people to screen their wellbeing progressively, prompting a more proactive way to deal with prosperity.

The difficulties in this space are focused on moral worries, information security, and fair admittance to these advancements. Adjusting the potential for further developed wellbeing results with the need to safeguard patient information and guarantee medical care openness stays a complicated undertaking.

Clean Energy and Manageability

The quest for clean energy arrangements is basic for tending to ecological difficulties. Advancements in sustainable power advancements, for example, sunlight based and wind power, are taking critical steps in diminishing our dependence on petroleum products. Energy capacity innovations, as cutting edge batteries, are empowering the proficient mix of environmentally friendly power sources into the framework.

Electric vehicles are changing the car business, lessening ozone harming substance discharges and air contamination. Also, propels in energy proficiency in structures and businesses add to supportability endeavors.

While the advancements in clean energy and manageability are promising, challenges stay as far as framework improvement, strategy support, and the change away from petroleum derivatives. Accomplishing a reasonable future requires an organized worldwide exertion and interest in green advancements.

Blockchain and Cryptographic money

Blockchain innovation, known for its part in supporting digital currencies like Bitcoin, has applications past the monetary area. Its decentralized and secure nature makes it reasonable for an extensive variety of purpose cases, from store network the board and casting a ballot frameworks to medical care information the executives and personality confirmation.

Digital currencies have likewise acquired conspicuousness as a potential disruptor in the conventional monetary industry. They offer the commitment of low exchange costs, expanded monetary consideration, and borderless exchanges. Nonetheless, administrative difficulties, worries about monetary solidness, and the requirement for purchaser security are critical obstacles that should be tended to.

Space Investigation and Commercialization

The space business is encountering a renaissance, driven by both government space organizations and privately owned businesses. Advancements in rocket innovation, satellite arrangement, and space the travel industry are extending the potential outcomes of room investigation and commercialization.

Privately owned businesses like SpaceX, Blue Beginning, and Virgin Cosmic are pushing the limits of what is attainable in space. They mean to decrease the expense of room access and, now and again, empower human colonization of different planets.

While the possibilities of room investigation and commercialization are invigorating, there are worries about space trash, the protection of divine bodies, and the moral ramifications of room exercises. As people adventure further into the universe, inquiries regarding planetary security and the dependable utilization of room assets become progressively significant.

Information Examination and Large Information

The wealth of information in this day and age has prompted the ascent of information examination and large information advances. Associations across businesses are utilizing information to acquire bits of knowledge into client conduct, functional productivity, and market patterns. Prescient investigation and AI are assisting organizations with settling on information driven choices and adjust to evolving conditions.

While large information offers the potential for huge business gains, it likewise presents difficulties connected with information protection, security, and the dependable utilization of information. Finding some kind of harmony between information driven advancement and moral information rehearses is a continuous undertaking.

Web of Things (IoT)

The Web of Things (IoT) alludes to the organization of interconnected gadgets and sensors that can gather and trade information. IoT is changing different businesses, from farming to medical services, by giving continuous data and empowering controller of gadgets.

In agribusiness, IoT sensors screen soil conditions and yield wellbeing, permitting ranchers to streamline water system and preparation. In medical care, IoT gadgets can remotely screen patient fundamental signs and give early alerts of medical problems.

In any case, the fast extension of IoT likewise raises worries about information security and protection. With additional gadgets gathering and communicating information, the gamble of information breaks and cyberattacks increments. Finding some kind of harmony between the advantages of IoT and the insurance of touchy information is critical.

Challenges and Moral Contemplations

As development and innovative progressions keep on reshaping our reality, they carry with them a bunch of mind boggling difficulties and moral contemplations. These difficulties incorporate issues like information protection, network safety, work dislodging, disparity, and ecological supportability.

Information protection is a huge worry as more private and delicate data is gathered and handled. Finding some kind of harmony between the advantages of information driven development and the need to safeguard people's protection is a sensitive errand.

Network safety is another major problem. As innovation propels, so do the capacities of noxious entertainers. Guaranteeing the security of advanced foundation and delicate information is of foremost significance.

Work uprooting because of computerization and simulated intelligence is a worry for the labor force. While innovative headways set out new open doors, they additionally render a few positions out of date. Guaranteeing a simply progress for impacted specialists and giving open doors to reskilling and upskilling is fundamental.

9.3 The Road Ahead: Sustaining Small Businesses for Tomorrow

Private ventures are the backbone of economies around the world, contributing essentially to work, development, and monetary development. Notwithstanding, the scene for private companies is continually developing, molded by a bunch of elements, including mechanical progressions, monetary variances, and changes in buyer conduct. To get their position from here on out, independent companies should adjust, develop, and beat different difficulties. In this article, we will investigate the street ahead for private companies and the procedures they can utilize to get by as well as flourish before very long.

Embracing Innovation and Computerized Change

One of the most pivotal components for the future outcome of private ventures is embracing innovation and going through advanced change. The quick speed of mechanical headway is consistently reshaping the manner in which organizations work. From online business and information examination to simulated intelligence and mechanization, innovation can possibly help productivity and seriousness.

Web based business, specifically, has turned into a distinct advantage for independent companies. Online commercial centers, virtual entertainment stages, and site retail facades offer independent companies the chance to grow their arrive at a long ways past their nearby geographic area. Organizations that put resources into making areas of strength for a presence can take advantage of a worldwide client base, expanding their income and potential open doors for development.

Additionally, embracing computer based intelligence and robotization can smooth out activities and diminish costs. Chatbots can deal with client requests, robotized stock administration can improve stock levels, and information examination can give important bits of knowledge into customer conduct. While carrying out innovation might include forthright expenses, the drawn out benefits as far as proficiency and intensity can far offset the underlying speculation.

Exploring Monetary Vulnerabilities

Private companies are frequently defenseless to financial changes, and the capacity to explore these vulnerabilities is basic for their supportability. Monetary slumps, for example, the one achieved by the Coronavirus pandemic, can present huge difficulties. To get their future, independent companies should focus on monetary preparation, broadening, and spryness.

Having a distinct monetary arrangement that incorporates cash holds and admittance to credit can assist independent companies with enduring financial tempests. Differentiating their income streams can likewise decrease weakness to monetary shocks. For instance, a café that depends exclusively on eat in clients might consider extending its takeout and conveyance administrations. Such broadening can assist with moderating the effect of limitations or lockdowns.

Readiness in adjusting to advertise shifts is one more urgent component for private companies. The capacity to turn rapidly and change their plan of action to suit changing conditions can be a life saver during monetary slumps. The pandemic, for example, constrained numerous private ventures to reconsider their tasks and track down innovative ways of keeping on serving their clients.

Manageability and Social Obligation

Manageability and social obligation are progressively significant elements in forming the fate of private companies. Customers are turning out to be more aware of natural and social issues, and organizations are supposed to line up with manageable practices. Manageability isn't just about being eco-accommodating; it additionally includes moral stock chains and fair work rehearses.

Private companies that focus on maintainability can draw in a developing section of eco-cognizant buyers and upgrade their standing on the lookout. Carrying out harmless to the ecosystem rehearses, for example, lessening waste, utilizing sustainable power sources, and obtaining morally created materials, could help the climate at any point as well as separate a business in a jam-packed market.

Besides, supporting social causes and exhibiting corporate social obligation can resound with shoppers. Private companies that participate in generous exercises or add to their nearby networks can fabricate generosity and encourage a feeling of imparted values to their clients.

Cooperation and Associations

In the interconnected universe of business, cooperation and associations are useful assets for private ventures to flourish from here on out. By cooperating with different associations, private ventures can get sufficiently close to new business sectors, advances, and mastery that may be trying to freely obtain.

Coordinated efforts can take different structures, from joint endeavors and co-showcasing endeavors to shared assets and information trade. For instance, a neighborhood pastry kitchen could team up with a close by café to offer a packaged breakfast bargain, helping the two organizations by drawing in a more extensive client base.

Associations can likewise stretch out past the nearby level. Private companies can join industry-explicit affiliations, organizations, or offices of trade to acquire bits of knowledge, influence aggregate bartering power, and promoter for arrangements that favor their inclinations.

Adjusting to Administrative Conditions

Administrative conditions assume a urgent part in molding the eventual fate of private companies. Legislatures lay out the guidelines and norms that organizations should comply with, which can fluctuate essentially by locale and industry. To guarantee consistence and keep away from legitimate issues and fines, private companies should remain informed about administrative changes and adjust to their particular settings.

Administrative consistence can be especially trying for private companies with restricted assets. This is where looking for lawful insight or cooperating with industry affiliations can give direction and backing. Remaining proactive and informed about administrative changes is a vital technique for exploring the perplexing scene of guidelines.

Admittance to Capital and Subsidizing

Admittance to capital is a persevering through worry for private ventures, and it stays a test from now on. While there are different wellsprings of financing accessible, for example, bank credits, funding, and crowdfunding, getting capital can be a huge obstacle for business visionaries.

Before very long, independent ventures might have to investigate elective funding choices. Influence money management, which consolidates monetary gets back with social and natural advantages, is acquiring noticeable quality. Shared loaning stages and microloans are extra roads for getting capital.

Local area based funding models likewise assume an essential part in supporting private companies. Local area banks and credit associations offer monetary help and are much of the time more open than bigger monetary establishments. Nearby speculation organizations and crowdfunding stages empower networks to help neighborhood adventures straightforwardly.

Adjusting to the Changing Idea of Work

The fate of work is going through a change, which has suggestions for independent companies. The ascent of remote and adaptable work courses of action gives the two open doors and difficulties. On the positive side, remote work can empower organizations to take advantage of a worldwide ability pool and diminish above costs related with actual office spaces.

Notwithstanding, overseeing remote groups and keeping areas of strength for a culture can more test. Independent companies need to adjust their administration and correspondence procedures to lead and connect with remote groups really. They should likewise think about the ramifications of remote work on network safety, information security, and representative prosperity.

Adjusting adaptability and construction will be fundamental for private companies in store for work. Guaranteeing that remote and in-office representatives can team up actually is imperative for efficiency and development.

Exploring a Serious Scene

The cutthroat scene is consistently developing for independent ventures. They face contest from other independent companies as well as from bigger partnerships and tech goliaths. The ascent of internet business and online commercial centers has made it simpler for shoppers to look at items and costs, which can put independent ventures in a difficult situation on the off chance that they can't offer cutthroat estimating and remarkable client care.

To stay serious, independent companies should zero in on their novel offers. This might include offering customized administrations, specialty items, or remarkable client encounters. Building a steadfast client base through trust and fulfillment will be basic for long haul achievement.

Development as an Upper hand

Development is the backbone of private companies, and it will keep on being a main thrust in their future. Independent ventures that enhance and adjust to changing client needs and market patterns are bound to flourish. Advancement doesn't necessarily need state of the art innovation; it can include process upgrades, imaginative promoting systems, or new item contributions.

Private companies ought to cultivate a culture of development, empowering representative imagination, and putting resources into innovative work. They can likewise take advantage of outside wellsprings of advancement, like associations with research establishments or support in startup hatcheries and gas pedals.